Clarence B. Bass

ETHICAL AND RELIGIOUS CLASSICS
OF EAST AND WEST
NO. II

THE THOUGHT OF THE PROPHETS

ETHICAL AND RELIGIOUS CLASSICS OF THE EAST AND WEST

RŪMĪ: POET AND MYSTIC
by Reynold A. Nicholson

SUFISM
by A. J. Arberry

SAINT FRANCIS IN ITALIAN PAINTING
by George Kaftal

THE MYSTICS OF SPAIN
by Allison Peers

THE POETRY AND CAREER OF LI PO
by Arthur Waley

SONGS OF ZARATHUSHTRA
by Dastur Framroze Ardeshir Bode and Piloo Nanavutty

AKBAR'S RELIGIOUS THOUGHT
by Emmy Wellesz

THE FAITH AND PRACTICE OF AL-GHAZALI
by W. Montgomery Watt

THE HOLY KORAN
by A. J. Arberry

PLOTINUS
by A. H. Armstrong

THE THOUGHT OF THE PROPHETS

By

Rabbi
ISRAEL I. MATTUCK
A. M. (Harvard)
Hon. D.H.L. (Hebrew Union College)

LONDON
GEORGE ALLEN AND UNWIN LTD
Ruskin House Museum Street

FIRST PUBLISHED 1953

PRINTED IN GREAT BRITAIN
in 11-point Baskerville type
BY C. TINLING AND CO. LTD
LIVERPOOL, LONDON AND PRESCOT

TO H. N. SPALDING

who encouraged me to write this book

GENERAL INTRODUCTION

As a result of two Wars that have devastated the World men and women everywhere feel a twofold need. We need a deeper understanding and appreciation of other peoples and their civilizations, especially their moral and spiritual achievements. And we need a wider vision of the Universe, a clearer insight into the fundamentals of ethics and religion. How ought men to behave? How ought nations? Does God exist? What is His Nature? How is He related to His creation? Especially, how can man approach Him? In other words, there is a general desire to know what the greatest minds, whether of East or West, have thought and said about the Truth of God and of the beings who (as most of them hold) have sprung from Him, live by Him, and return to Him.

It is the object of this Series, which originated among a group of Oxford men and their friends, to place the chief ethical and religious masterpieces of the world, both Christian and non-Christian, within easy reach of the intelligent reader who is not necessarily an expert—the ex-Service man who is interested in the East, the undergraduate, the adult student, the intelligent public generally. The Series will contain books of three kinds: translations, reproductions of ideal and religious art, and background books showing the surroundings in which the literature and art arose and developed. These books overlap each other. Religious art, both in East and West, often illustrates a religious text, and in suitable cases the text and the pictures will be printed together to complete each other. The background books will often consist largely of translations. The volumes will be prepared by scholars of distinction, who will try to make them, not only scholarly, but intelligible and enjoyable. This Introduction represents the views of the General Editors as to the scope of the Series, but not necessarily the views of all contributors to it. The contents of the books will also be very varied—ethical and social, biographical, devotional, philosophic and mystical, whether in poetry, in pictures or in prose. There is a great wealth of material. Confucius lived in a time much like our own, when State was at war with State and the people suffering and disillusioned; and the 'Classics' he preserved or inspired show the social virtues that may unite families, classes and States into one great family, in obedience to the Will of Heaven. Asoka and Akbar (both of them great patrons of art) ruled a vast Empire on the principles of religious faith. There are the moral anecdotes and moral maxims of the Jewish and Muslim writers of the Middle Ages. There are the beautiful tales of courage, love and fidelity in the Indian and Persian epics. Shakespeare's plays show that he thought the true relation between man and man is love. Here and there a volume will illustrate the unethical or less ethical man and difficulties that beset him.

Then there are the devoted and philosophic works. The lives and legends (legends often express religious truth with clarity and beauty) of the Buddha, of the parents of Mary, of Francis of Assisi, and the exquisite sculptures and paintings that illustrate them. Indian and Christian religious music, and the words of prayer and praise which the music intensifies. There are the prophets and apocalyptic writers, Zarathustrian and Hebrew; the Greek philosophers, Christian thinkers—and the Greek, Latin, medieval and modern—whom they so deeply influenced. There is, too, the Hindu, Buddhist and Christian teaching expressed in such great monuments as the Indian temples, Barabudur (the Chartres of Asia) and Ajanta, Chartres itself and the Sistine Chapel.

Finally there are the mystics of feeling, and the mystical philosophers. In God-loving India the poets, musicians, sculptors and painters inspired by the spiritual worship of Krishna and Rama, as well as the philosophic mystics from the Upanishads onward. The two great Taoists Lao-tze and Chuang-tze and the Sung mystical painters in China, Rumi and other sufis in Islam, Plato and Plotinus, followed by 'Dionysius', Eckhart, St. John of the Cross and (in our view) Dante and other great mystics and mystical painters in many Christian lands.

Mankind is hungry, but the feast is there, though it is locked up and hidden away. It is the aim of this Series to put it within reach, so that, like the heroes of Homer, we may stretch forth our hands to the good cheer laid before us.

No doubt the great religions differ in fundamental respects. But they are not nearly so far from one another as they seem. We think they are further off than they are largely because we so often misunderstand and misrepresent them. Those whose own religion is dogmatic have often been as ready to learn from other teachings as those who are liberals in religion. Above all, there is an enormous amount of common ground in the great religions, concerning, too, the most fundamental matters. There is frequent agreement on the Divine Nature; God is the One, Self-subsisting Reality, knowing Himself, and therefore loving and rejoicing in Himself. Nature and finite spirits are in some way subordinate kinds of Being, or merely appearances of the Divine, the One. The three stages of the way of man's approach or return to God are in essence the same in Christian and non-Christian teaching: an ethical stage, then one of knowledge and love, leading to the mystical union of the soul with God. Each stage will be illustrated in these volumes.

Something of all this may (it is hoped) be learnt from the books and pictures in this Series. Read and pondered with a desire to learn, they will help men and women to find 'fullness of life', and peoples to live together in greater understanding and harmony. To-day the earth is beautiful, but men are disillusioned and afraid. But there may come a day, perhaps not a distant day, when there will be a renaissance of man's spirit: when men will be innocent and happy amid the beauty of the world, or their eyes will be opened to see that egoism and strife are folly, that the universe is fundamentally spiritual, and that men are the sons of God.

> They shall not hurt nor destroy
> In all My holy mountain:
> For all the earth shall be full of the
> knowledge of the Lord
> As the waters cover the sea.

THE EDITORS

PREFACE

The Biblical quotations are taken from the Revised version with occasional changes intended to clarify the meaning of a verse or to reproduce more nearly the connotation of a word or phrase in the original. The notation of chapters and verses follows the English Bible. Transliterated Hebrew and Greek words are put in italics.

I owe thanks to Professor Sheldon N. Black of the Hebrew Union College, Cincinnati, U.S.A., who read the typescript, and I adopted a number of his suggestions. I also owe thanks to Mr. John Rayner who read the proofs and prepared the indices.

I explain in the Introduction the method I followed in interpreting the thought of the Prophets. It need only be added that the limitation in the size of the book prevented me from presenting all the evidence for my statements, or to discuss in detail the passages which I quote. But since the book is intended for the general reader, these omissions may also be justified by its purpose.

I. I. M.

CONTENTS

INTRODUCTION

The Prophets in the subject of this book are those whose teachings have been preserved in the prophetic books of the Hebrew Bible. They hold a supremely important place in the history of Judaism. They moulded its distinctive character, using, it is true, older material, but in such a way as to make it serve a radical development of thought. That applies especially to the Prophets of the 8th and 7th centuries, B.C., who implanted in Judaism the ideas which differentiated it fundamentally from the other religions of antiquity, and enabled the ancient Hebrews to survive a national destruction like that which ended completely the history of many other small ancient nations. The towering place which these Prophets hold in the religious history of the Jews gives their thought an historic interest, not only for Judaism but also for the two religions descended from it, Christianity and Islam.

Their thought has, however, more than an historic interest. The fact that their books are used now, as they have been used for many centuries in the Western world, in worship and religious instruction, warrants the inference that their thought has permanent relevance to the human situation. Its present religious significance does not always lie on the surface of their utterances. Their world was quite different from ours; they put their thought in a different framework of ideas. Not all their utterances can, therefore, have, literally, present relevance; some of them were too closely related to the general thought of their time to survive it, or too much bound up with their special circumstances to fit our circumstances. But many of their utterances express ideas which transcend the circumstances that evoked them and break through the framework of thought which gave them their form. So, prophecies addressed to Israel have universal meaning. It is the aim of this book to present the ideas of the Prophets in a way which might show their permanent relevance to all human life and thought.

The task of interpreting the Prophets is confronted with some danger and several difficulties. The danger attends every effort of interpretation; it is the danger of subjectivity, which is aggravated for a study of the Prophets by their method. They were not philosophers, though a system of thought is implied in their teachings; their ideas are interrelated, but not presented in a system. They had a mighty faith and an urgent moral zeal. In the expression of their faith they enunciated, or implied when they did not enunciate, general religious ideas, and in the exercise of their moral zeal they implied general principles in dealing with particular situations. It is by attending to these general ideas and principles that, I think, we may derive from the Prophets permanent religious guidance both for thought and practice.

But they must be inferred from judgments on particular events or facts. That entails the necessity to analyse the significance of a judgment in the specific circumstances to which it is addressed and to uncover its implication in the contemporary framework of thought. To get at the present significance of the Prophets' ideas, it is, therefore, necessary not only to translate their language into ours but also to translate their particular judgments into the general ideas which they imply. For example, the Prophets often admonished kings, condemning actions which they judged wrong and urging actions which they deemed necessary for righteousness. Their country, like all countries at that time, was ruled by an absolute monarch. The king was the government. In the admonitions, therefore, which the Prophets addressed to kings they enunciated religious principles for government, and implied a political philosophy with a religious basis. What that philosophy was can be found only by analysing the significance of their sermons to kings in the thought framework and in the conditions of their time.

The process offers a large scope for error; the interpreter may be misled by the desire to have the support of the Prophets for his own ideas; but the danger cannot be avoided. We have to use our minds to get into their minds and our experience to understand the words in which they recount their experience. But we may not read into their words our ideas. It is true that the significance of an utterance may extend beyond the intention of its author, but the extension may not alter the original meaning, or its essential idea. The idea underlying a judgment on a particular situation may legitimately be applied in a very different situation; but its essential significance may not be changed. This method of interpreting the Prophets excludes reading into their words prognostications of future events, or ideas which they could not possibly have had. It must be distinguished from that followed by traditional theology which found in the Bible generally authority for later theological dogmas, and in the Prophets' statements about near events prognostications of later events which received a theological import. It must also be distinguished from the homiletical method which merely uses words of the Bible to convey the preacher's thought.

There is a related, and subtler, danger; that is, to look at the Prophets' thought with the eyes of a later theology, so that categories are applied to it which, unconsciously, prepare the ground for later beliefs. I venture to think that the excessive emphasis which some scholars put on personality in the Prophets' conception of God illustrates that danger. The inviolable condition for the interpretation of the Prophets is to begin with scrupulous attention to the meaning of their utterances in the circumstances which evoked them and their significance in the general contemporary framework of thought.

Other books in the Bible can be used only to a limited extent for an understanding of the Prophets. They were originators, influenced, undoubtedly, by what went before them, but not reproducing it. They influenced fundamentally the development of Judaism after them, but not everything in that development reproduced exactly their thought. The differences between their thought and the Hebrew religion before them, and between their thought and later developments, necessitate caution in the use of other parts of the Bible, though they do not completely prevent it, as a guide to the meaning which the Prophets gave to crucial words.

Several technical difficulties confront the study of the Prophets. The Hebrew text of their books is sometimes uncertain where an important idea may be involved. I have thought it best not to use such passages except when scholars generally agree on an emended text. Another difficulty is presented by the frequent uncertainty about the historical situation to which a prophecy is addressed. Sometimes it is even uncertain whether it refers to the past, present or future; verbs in Hebrew have no tenses, the time to which a verb refers must be deduced from the context. The Prophets aggravate the grammatical uncertainty by frequently treating the future as a completed present. Fortunately the salient facts in the historical situation to which a prophecy refers can most often be deduced from it.

Another difficulty is raised by the possibility of diverse and divergent interpretations of the same passage. That difficulty recurs frequently. An outstanding, and important example is Amos' attitude to monotheism. In such cases I have been compelled to decide which interpretation to follow, and to give the reason for my view. There is still a further difficulty which confronts especially the task undertaken in this book—the diversity among the Prophets. We speak of them collectively; but they were individuals diverse in temperament, circumstances, and thought. They did not all have the same ideas on every subject. A conspectus of their thought must take account of the differences and disagreements and relate them to their fundamental agreements.

On the other hand, to deal with the Prophets collectively avoids to some extent the frequent questions of authorship. To find the thought of a particular Prophet requires decisions as to what he wrote; but a synoptic view of the thought of the Prophets can, within limits, ignore questions of the authorship of specific passages. Such questions, however, must be answered when they also involve conclusions about ideas or principles which can be held together. It is, for example, important for an understanding of the thought of the Prophets to decide whether the hopeful prophecy at the end of the Book of Micah is by the same Prophet who in the rest of the book prophesied doom. It would retain some significance for the thought of the Prophets even if another Prophet wrote it, but its significance is enhanced if it belongs to Micah's thought. For the most part, however, questions of authorship, which, like questions of date, may be important for the history of ancient Israel, need not interfere with the understanding of the thought of the Prophets.

It should be added that the importance of the Prophets for religion lies not only in their ideas but also in themselves. Their prophetic consciousness, the sense of a mission imposed on them by divine inspiration, which gave them their distinctive greatness, has a significance for the general religious attitude. In few can the religious experience attain the fullness which it attained in them, but wherever it exists it has something of the same quality. Their contribution to religion consists of their thought and their experience.

ONE

THE NATURE OF THE PROPHETS

In the 8th century B.C. a new kind of prophet appeared among the Hebrews. There had always been prophets among them, men who claimed to be channels of communication from God. They were, therefore, used to draw on divine omniscience for a knowledge of the future or the hidden. Not without some success, it would seem, if the stories preserved in the Books of Samuel and Kings have an historic basis. Saul learnt from Samuel the whereabouts of his father's lost asses (I. Samuel: 9). Jehoshaphat asked Elisha to predict the outcome of a military campaign (II. Kings: 3 : 11ff). Sometimes prophets of this kind would induce a state of trance in themselves, at other times a state of ecstasy, the one a condition of repose, the other a condition of excitement; perhaps in one a waiting or receptive subconsciousness, in the other an active, or dominating, super-consciousness. In both, it was believed, the mind or spirit was fully opened to communications from God, so that what prophets spoke was taken as a message from Him. They were paid for their services; prophecy was their profession. Those who exercised it formed themselves into guilds. These prophets left no writings, only legends which adorn history with imagination, adding miracles to facts, to report the impression made by their activities and personalities. The Prophets of the 8th century, and later, resorted to writing.

Unlike the professional prophets they did not earn

their living by prophecy; they were always critical, and sometimes even scornful, of the professional prophets. Amos, when the high priest, angered by his threats of doom, bade him go elsewhere to prophesy 'for his bread', retorted: 'I am not a prophet, nor the son of a prophet' (a member of a guild of prophets) (Amos 7: 14). Yet in another context (Amos 3: 7) he claims to be a prophet. There is an apparent, but not a real, inconsistency. He was not a prophet of the kind the priest thought, one who prophesied for a living, but he was a prophet who spoke under a sense of compulsion from God. He was not a professional seer, one of those whom anxious people consulted, and paid, nor did he belong to any one of their guilds. But he spoke in the name of God, basing his claim to inspiration not on professional training, but on inner illumination and a sense of irresistible impulsion. Though he could not call himself a prophet in the old sense, he was a spokesman of God, a prophet, with another conception of the prophet's function. The professional prophet was used by men to get what they wanted from God, the other kind of prophet was used by God to tell men what He wanted from them. He was a teacher of religion.

There were in the earlier period of Jewish history prophets devoted to religious teaching and work. Elijah strove to establish among the Hebrews loyalty to their God with uncompromising exclusion of the worship of the Canaanite deities and the rites which went with them. Nathan and Elijah upbraided kings for wrong-doing. Some of the early prophets exercised a political function, which pertained to theocracy. Samuel and Elisha made and removed kings. The later Prophets, who left us their writings, continued the theocratic function.

Very little is known about the personal lives of most of them. Jeremiah's book, probably because a considerable part was written by his amanuensis, contains a number of biographical details which give a fairly extensive, though far from complete, account of his life. Other books of the Prophets contain notes of isolated experiences. Some of the Prophets have not even left their names. This lack of personal information about the Prophets has some significance for an understanding of the spirit of Judaism. Not in the Prophets as persons, but in their instruction, God revealed Himself. They did not claim a divine quality for themselves but divine inspiration, and therefore, divine authority, for what they said.

Behind the claim to divine inspiration lay an intense overpowering experience, the experience of a compelling pressure on, or in, their consciousness. Amos refers to it to justify his prophesying. Why should he, who was not a professional prophet, incur the odium, and the danger, of prophesying doom? The answer is: irresistible impulsion. He does it because he is compelled to do it. Compelled by whom? There can only be one answer: By Him who is behind all the phenomena in the universe—God (Amos 3: 8 and 7: 15). The Prophets had the consciousness of being dominated by God. Jeremiah describes the experience simply and poignantly: God has overmastered him. In spite of his natural shyness, and the reluctance of his sensitive nature to face contumely and personal animosity, he must speak out. 'O Lord, thou hast (irresistibly) persuaded me, and I was persuaded; thou art stronger than I, and hast prevailed: I am become a laughing stock all the day, every one mocketh me. For as often as I speak, I cry out: I cry, Violence and spoil: because the word of the Lord is made a reproach unto me, and a derision, all the day. And if I say, I will not make mention of him, nor speak any more in his name, then there is in mine heart, as it were, a burning fire shut up in my bones, and I am weary with forbearing, I cannot contain' (Jeremiah 20: 7-9). The feeling of compulsion proved to the Prophets that God had 'laid his hand' on them, that His spirit was pressing on theirs with an irresistible urgency (Isaiah 8: 11, Ezekiel 1: 3, 3: 14).

The experience had a mystical quality. It brought an intense awareness of God, like that which made some mystics feel completely absorbed in Him. The Prophets were not mystics in that sense; they could not, in the framework of their thought, have so exalted, or transfigured, their humanity. But they were wholly pervaded by that intense feeling of immediate communion with God which lies at the heart of all mysticism. They were mystics in the sense that they experienced God immediately, without anything between Him and them, with the whole of their being. They gave themselves to Him and He filled them with His spirit.

They translated the revelation that came to them in their mystic communion with God into auditory terms. They heard Him. 'And the Lord of Hosts revealed himself in mine ears' (Isaiah 22: 14a cf. Isaiah 21: 10). Several of the Prophets report that their ministries began with a kind of vision. Isaiah recounts that after the death of the king, with whom he seems to have been a favourite, he went into the Temple where, in a haze, he became aware of God and the heavenly host, and heard a voice calling for someone to take God's message to the people of Judah; and he, though hesitant because of his unworthiness, undertook the mission. Jeremiah records that when he was still young he was appointed to the prophetic mission which he was compelled to accept in spite of his youth and reluctance. 'Then the Lord put forth his hand, and touched my mouth; and the Lord said unto me, Behold, I have put my words into thy mouth' (Jeremiah 1: 9). Ezekiel tells that he received, in a trance when he saw heaven, God and His angelic hosts, a scroll which he was made to eat, containing the message he was to preach, with the summons to stand on his feet as the representative of the human race, and to proclaim the word of God. These and other Prophets report similar visions in the course of their ministries (e.g. Isaiah 21: 6-9; Ezekiel 8; Amos 7: 6-9; Zechariah 1: 7; 2: 5 and 5: 1 to 6: 8). The significance of these reports cannot be assessed with sufficient certainty to base on them any generalisation about the nature of prophecy. Some of the visions may describe actual experiences, others might be literary devices to express in concrete form an abstract idea, or—more often—an intense feeling. In any case, the significance of a vision lies not in itself but in the underlying mystic experience. That experience may move from the field of actuality into that of imagination, sometimes consciously and sometimes unconsciously. Its intensity obliterates the dividing line between subjective and objective. The mysticism of the Prophets showed itself not in visions but in their prophesying.

Some of the Prophets do not report any mystic visions. Hosea and Micah plainly indicate that the impulsion to the prophetic ministry came to them through ordinary experiences heightened to an extraordinary intensity. Though Amos reports visions during his ministry, it did not begin with a vision. In his lonely meditations, moved and filled with the awesome and lonely silence of the wilderness, he heard the inner call to warn the people of the doom impending over them, because of their sinful ways and their violation of God's law in their dealings with one another. Hosea said that he learnt about the way of God's love for Israel from the way he, or another man, would treat, or had treated, an unfaithful wife. Micah was moved by the sad and sometimes tragic experiences of impoverished farmers, who were oppressed by the rich and the strong, to denounce existing social conditions and to plead for social reform. The word 'vision' or 'saw' occurs in the headings of several of the books of the Prophets, but they had become technical terms for the utterances of prophets, not necessarily descriptive of their experiences. The mystic experience does not necessarily involve, or bring, visions. It may come in deep meditation when men can be filled with the sense of the immediate and, as it were, full presence of God. 'Mysticism' is frequently used in the sense of an abnormal, or supranormal, experience in which men perceive details in the mysteries of heaven or earth. That was not the mysticism of the Prophets; theirs was the mysticism of a personal experience of God raised to such an intensity that they felt themselves so identified—not identical—with Him that they could claim to be one with Him.

They reached the spiritual and moral heights to which human personality can attain under the influence of a Power more than human. They were so steeped in God that He was in the very warp and woof of their personality, dominating their thinking and their feeling. They identified themselves with Him in such a way that they had no interests apart from Him. Knowing God meant to them not merely an intellectual apprehension of His existence, but such a complete personal relation with Him, a union so intimate and close, that not a word was spoken but it came from Him, not an action performed but He was the mover. When they spoke of God, they seemed at times to move, unconsciously, between the third person and the first, from 'He (God) said' to 'I said', or introducing what they said with 'God said'. Isaiah begins a sermon to the king with 'The Lord spake to Ahaz' (Isaiah 7: 10). Jeremiah ascribes his own feelings to God (Jeremiah 31: 20). It is not merely anthropomorphism. Because of the sense of identification (not identity) with God, the Prophets could claim effective power for their words, for they were not their, but God's, words. What may sound like a super-arrogant boast, when Jeremiah says that he has been appointed 'to pluck up and break down, and to destroy and to overthrow, to build, and to plant' (Jeremiah 1: 10 cf. 31: 28), simply expressed the Prophet's consciousness. He is a channel for God's power, an instrument in the hand of God; sometimes an unwilling, a hesitant, or even rebellious instrument. His identification with God does not imply a claim to divinity or to superhuman power. He does what God wills, he says what God thinks.

The Prophets remained in the framework of human life. Their mysticism did not imply a supernatural quality in their lives. They would themselves have firmly objected to the attitude which put them in a category apart from other men. They shared in our common humanity, so that they revealed its high potentialities. All men can have in some measure the knowledge of God which they had in a high degree. They refute the psychology which reduces man and his impulses wholly to physical instincts. That psychology crumbles in the presence of spiritual greatness. The element of mystery in the Prophets can be coarsened but not explained by its theories. And there is no difference in kind between the humanity of the Prophets and the humanity of ordinary men. That is the significance in the apparent stress on Moses' ordinary humanity in the verse 'the man Moses was humble indeed' (Numbers 12: 3).

Nor did the Prophets' mysticism empty them of their human traits. The mystic does not break all contact with his thought or character. He remains within the compass of his personality. When he identifies himself with God, it is he, not an empty shell, that is taken up into the identification. In the result, his personality may be transformed, his past experiences reveal their deeper meaning, his reasoned thought raised to an apprehension beyond reason, but they all have a part in the mystical experience. The human element in it detracts from its perfection, but enhances its value, it remains a human experience. The divine and human are fused in it. If the divine enters into the fusion with less than itself, the human is raised by it to more than itself.

The human element in the mystical experience not only explains the diversity in the ways the mystics have described it, but it also produces diversity in the forms and contents of the experience. So, though the Prophets were mystics and their prophesying was stimulated and fed by mystical experiences, their diverse characters, attainments and pursuits produced diversity in the ways they expressed their thought. Amos and Micah were stern, Hosea was gentle, Jeremiah was tender and sensitive. Isaiah was commanding, and Ezekiel almost suave. They lived diverse lives. Amos was an agricultural worker, given to meditation under the impact of nature's awesome order.

Micah was a farmer, stung by the injustices which turned the farmer's life into a misery. Hosea was a town aristocrat, sensitive to the joys which love can give and to the pains it can inflict. Isaiah was a courtier, one of the king's friends and entourage, moved to more than a political interest in political events. Jeremiah and Ezekiel were educated priests, who judged divergently the priestly rites, one condemning them as a perversion of the service which God requires, the other prescribing their details so as to make them fully expressive of the worship of God. Being diverse in temperament, the Prophets received their revelations diversely, and used diverse idioms to express the consequent ideas. Being like other men, they expressed themselves in what they said, but being Prophets, they received instruction from God.

Their mysticism was distinguished by its ethical quality. They must have found spiritual satisfaction in the fullness of their experience of God. There is a hint of it here and there in their writings. 'Thy words were found, and I did eat them; and thy words were unto me a joy and the rejoicing of mine heart: for I am called by thy name, O Lord God of hosts' (Jeremiah 15: 16). Though the prophetic mission, and the trouble it entailed, made Jeremiah curse the day of his birth (Jeremiah 20: 14), yet he found joy in the experience which imposed the mission on him. The joy was in the experience, the trouble came afterwards because it forced him to denounce irreligion and unrighteousness. The ethical significance of the Prophets' mystical experience fills their writings. When they experienced God intensely they felt the intense pressure of His righteousness. The mystical experience, therefore, brought moral intensity. They brought to it a moral and social idealism which it clarified in the light from God and kindled into a burning social and moral passion.

The Prophets do not themselves claim, nor did others claim for them, that they performed miracles.[1] If any evidence were needed that miracles are an accretion to, not an element in, the lives of great religious teachers they supply it conclusively. Isaiah offered King Ahaz a sign, but the sign he gave was only the prediction that within two or three years the kings who threatened to invade Judah would lose their kingdoms (Isaiah 7). The Prophets predicted events not as the seers did who claimed to foresee the future, but by applying the laws by which, in their thought, God ruled the course of human lives and human history. What they said about the future issued from their teaching about God and His moral law.

The Prophets used, in the first place, the spoken word and symbolic action to carry their message. At one time or another in the course of their ministries they felt constrained to resort to writing. Jeremiah gives his reason; he wanted to continue, while in prison, his preaching to the king and people. 'And Jeremiah commanded Baruch saying, I am shut up; I cannot go into the house of the Lord; therefore go thou, and read in the scroll, which thou hast written from my mouth, the words of the Lord in the ears of the people in the Lord's house upon the fast day; and also thou shalt read them in the ears of all Judah that come out of their cities' (Jeremiah 36: 5-6). But he also had, seemingly, a long range motive with two aspects. By its permanence a book might, soon or late, achieve what the spoken word failed to accomplish. With the Prophet's admonitions constantly dinned into them by reading, the people might be brought to

[1] Isaiah 38:7f can only be a later legendary invention.

repentance. 'Take thee (addressed to his amanuensis, Baruch) a scroll, and write therein all the words I have spoken unto thee against Israel, and against Judah, and against all the nations, from the day I spake unto thee, from the days of Josiah, even unto this day. It may be that the house of Judah will hear all the evil which I purpose to do unto them; that they may return every man from his evil way; that I may forgive their iniquity and their sin' (Jeremiah 36: 2-3).[1] If, however, the people persisted in their heedlessness to the Prophet's admonitions, and consequently calamity would overtake them, his book would be there to prove the truth of his prophecy. Isaiah may express similar motives for committing his sermons to writing (Isaiah 8: 16 and 30: 8).

The books of the Prophets are largely in poetry. It may be accepted that they also spoke in poetry, it was their natural mode of expression. They were poets as well as preachers. It is doubtful whether they ever spoke in a condition of ecstatic excitement. Occasionally one of them may have acted ecstatically (Isaiah 20: 2f, though it is hard to believe that the Prophet went naked for three years; a texual error, or legend making exaggeration, may have stretched a very brief time, like three hours,[2] into an unbelievable exaggeration); but their books do not give any evidence of ecstatic speech. They spoke rationally, without frenzy, but passionately. They received their inspiration in trances or through deep meditation; but they moulded their instruction by thought.

The part which reason played in the thought of the

[1] Note that the first person refers at first to the Prophet and in the second verse to God.

[2] The Hebrew word for hours might easily be mistaken for the word which means years.

Prophets is shown both by the rational form of their prophecies and the rationality of their contents. While they introduce their exhortations with 'Thus saith the Lord', they often appeal to reason. They give a rational ground for their claim to be true prophets.[1] When Isaiah says that God pleads with the people 'let us reason together', he gives reason a place in his apprehension of God and His ways. And when all the Prophets support their plea for loyalty to God with arguments drawn from nature, human life and human history, they imply the authority of reason. But at the same time they show an emphatic awareness of its inadequacy for the full knowledge of God, which is the utmost apprehension of reality and truth. 'For my ways are not your ways, and my thoughts are not your thoughts, saith the Lord' (Isaiah 55: 8-9). So they 'wait on God', seeking through concentrated communion with Him to receive the illumination which would give their reason more than reason's light (Jeremiah 42: 1-7).

The central idea in the Prophets' thought is that God is the Sovereign of the universe, acting in a moral order which expresses, and embodies, His righteousness. The idea was new. They attained to it by inspiration, but they were prepared for it by experience, and they interpreted it by reason. Mystical experience and ethical reasoning combined to produce their message. They used their reason, but the heavens opened to reveal its truth to them. The truth came to them as in a flash, and it burnt in them constantly with an unquenchable and irresistible fire.

Micah may guide us to the central point in the Prophets' experience which galvanised them into the consciousness of a divine mission. It flared up out of

[1] See pages 38ff.

the friction between two conflicting facts. On the one hand, there was in the Prophets such an intense awareness of God, His justice and His love, that it filled their whole being, dominating their thoughts and emotions. On the other hand, there was the life they saw among men: luxury for the rich and misery for the poor, deceit and treachery, indifference to religion, and the practice of idolatry. The world and God were in conflict, and the conflict held the threat of doom. The threat was in some cases underlined, emphasised, or brought very near, by a present or imminent calamity, like an impending invasion of Palestine or a plague of locusts. There was only one way to avoid or to survive it; to remove the conflict with God. That was the mission which took hold of the Prophets in their intense experience of God and His righteousness.

The Prophets spoke to the Hebrews but their thought took the nations, which they knew, individually and all mankind collectively within its purview. Israel was the centre of their world, but the whole world was their concern as it was the concern of the One God. The Prophets felt, therefore, that they were commissioned to preach to the nations as well as to the Jews. Jeremiah says that he was appointed 'a prophet to the nations' (Jeremiah 1: 5). In the allegory of the Book of Jonah, God sends a prophet to Nineveh to preach repentance, the same message that all the Prophets gave to Israel. The prophecies in nearly all the books of the Prophets about, or to, the nations show that they interpreted with a universal scope their mission to spread the knowledge of God and His law.

TWO

THE AUTHORITY OF THE PROPHETS

A MYSTERY must haunt the study of the Prophets. Because their ideas have become the truisms of religious thought, there appears to be nothing original in their teachings. But in their time their monotheism was new. Their thought begins with the belief in One God and ends in Him. His reality is for them the fundamental fact of all existence; and to attain a knowledge of Him, the goal of men's existence. Before them, Judaism itself, though it demanded the worship of one God, admitted the existence of other gods, and all other religions were polytheistic. The Prophets' idea that religion required not sacrifices and rites, but righteousness, was also new. They raised morality to a paramount place in the good life at a time when religion generally ignored it or underrated its religious importance. The passion with which they preached righteousness as a religious duty, an obligation imposed by God, and the way to worship Him, gave their moral teaching originality and distinction in their time and gives it power for all time.

Moreover, their originality was enhanced by their insistence that the righteousness which God required exceeded in its demands accepted moral standards. It would not, I think, be realistic to infer from the Prophets' denunciations of the spiritual and moral conditions of their time that there was widespread corruption, that all the people stubbornly or thoughtlessly pursued wicked ways in defiance of the normal morality of their time. Some corruption there undoubtedly was; as at all times and among all peoples, there were some who violated the generally accepted moral standards. They vitiated the life of the community, especially if they held high places. These were wicked men, and despotic rulers; and the Prophets denounced them. But present observation and recorded history give ground for the generalisation that most people abide by the prevailing morality of their time. The Prophets directed their invective largely against the inadequacy of its standards, against the immorality of conventional morality, against low commercial practices and poor ethical conduct which were accepted as normal. The good men were not good enough; their conception of righteousness was inadequate, thin, poor.[1] The good, as it has often been said, is the enemy of the best; and the Prophets wanted passionately the best. An inadequate conception of righteousness prevents the development of a more righteous world. Moral lethargy, even more than wickedness, because it is both more prevalent and more persistent, blocks the way to the Kingdom of God.

The social facts which the Prophets stigmatised were not recognised as evils but as the normal concomitants of the existing social order. They were judged right according to its standards. But the Prophets condemned the facts as evils; the standards which approved or accepted them were wrong; the social order which allowed or supported them did not comport with the righteousness of God. Their experience of God impressed on them the urgent need for higher standards. Ordinary people could not be con-

[1] May this be the meaning of Micah 7:4, "The best of them is as a brier: the most upright is worse than a thorn hedge the day of thy watchmen, even thy visitation is come, now shall be their perplexity."

vinced that the evils should, and could, be removed. They seemed to accept existing conditions and the standards that approved them. 'Then I said, Surely these are poor; they are foolish; for they know not the way of the Lord, nor the judgment of their God. What, then? 'I will get me unto the great men, and will speak unto them; for they know the way of the Lord and the judgment of their God. But these with one accord have broken the yoke, and burst the bands' (Jeremiah 5: 4-5). Alas! the great and the learned, who know, or ought to know, the moral requirements of religion, also accept the evils. The people lack knowledge, but the priests are like the people (Hosea 4: 6 and 9).

How did the Prophets discover the new ideas which they enunciated? They were original and revolutionary. Their own answer is clear: God revealed them to us. But the way of revelation must remain a mystery. For themselves their all absorbing relation to God justified the conviction, which it generated, that they were channels of His revelation. By their complete devotion to Him they opened themselves to Him, so that they attributed to His illumination their knowledge of Him, all that it included, and all that followed from it. The intensity of their experience of God verified for them the content of their thought and teaching. Their warrant was their consciousness of an inescapable mission. My message, said Amos, is my credentials; it proves that God has sent me. Every event has a cause; his life as a shepherd had taught him that. When the lion roars, he has spied his prey; when a trap springs, it has been touched off. When the Prophet speaks, it is because God impels him. The Prophets did not support their instruction by quoting a book, or justify their demands by appeals to a formal tradition. Their intuitive apprehension of the righteousness of God may have been stimulated by the best tradition in Judaism. In all religions a distinction has to be made, unfortunately, between what many call tradition and the real tradition which they often ignore. The story of Nathan's condemnation of David for his treatment of Uriah, Elijah's rebuke to Ahab over Naboth's vineyard, the story of Abraham's plea with God for Sodom and Gomorrah (Shall the God of justice be unjust?), and the oldest laws in the Pentateuch show that already in its earliest development, Judaism gave an important place to divine and human righteousness in its teaching. Though that aspect of Judaism was often obscured by ritual demands, it maintained itself by its own power, and may well have exercised a paramount influence on the Prophets of the books. But they did not base their teaching on an authoritative tradition. Nor did they possess any authority conferred on them by an official status. The priests relied on codes of laws, written or transmitted by word of mouth. The instructions they gave derived authority from their priestly office. The Prophets, on the other hand, had no official status. They spoke 'with authority', the authority of inspiration: 'Thus saith the Lord'.

Looking back at them from this long distance of time, we find justification for their claim to divine inspiration in the truth and originality of their fundamental ideas. The originality is a fact of history; the truth has been proved in the growing spiritual and moral attainments of mankind. Events which they foretold did not always happen, but principles which led to their predictions were valid, even when the predictions were wrong; and the principles were their chief concern. They were religious teachers, dominated by an urgent sense of the mission to teach men about God and the way of righteousness. Their passionate utterances about Him and His law have the ring of truth and have been proved true.

For their contemporaries their claim to inspiration was not enough to establish their authority. They implicitly brought in reason to support it. They imposed a rational test on prophecy itself. They condemned as 'false prophets' others who also claimed to be inspired but who, unlike them, prophesied 'smooth' things. Conceivably, those who preached that all was well might have been actuated by the sincere belief that they were expressing the will of God. When men, calling themselves prophets, contradicted Jeremiah's emphatic assertion that the nation would be destroyed if it did not reform, they might have sincerely felt that they were speaking the truth. By saying what the people liked to hear, they roused the suspicion of insincerity for the sake of applause or profit. The true prophet must be on guard against mere compliance with popular views or wishes. 'Say ye not, A conspiracy, concerning all whereof this people shall say, A conspiracy, neither fear ye their fear, nor be in dread thereof' (Isaiah 8: 12). Those who should lead the people are too often tempted to follow popular clamour and the short-lived—because not founded on moral judgment—enthusiasm of the masses. On the other hand, preachers might proclaim that all will be well with sincere conviction. The author of the second part of the Book of Isaiah did so. He lived, however, in the 6th century B.C. in Babylonia, when the threats of destruction uttered by the earlier prophets had been fulfilled and the people hungered for hope. But the circumstances in Jeremiah's time, judged religiously, precluded an optimistic view of the immediate future. The people had fallen below the spiritual apprehension and the moral conduct that true religion required. The moral situation, in several ways, violated the rule of God. Disaster must follow.

The Prophets used contemporaneous events to enforce their judgment. Destruction was on the way, it was imminent. They were impelled by a sense of crisis. Isaiah faced the king, with what was probably his first prophetic utterance, when Judea was threatened by invasion. The report of invading Scythian hosts, moving southward from their home in the north in a succession of conquests, evoked Jeremiah's first prophecy. The history of ancient Palestine consisted of recurring crises. It lay in the centre of its world, so that ambitious monarchs sent their armies into it and across it in their pursuit of imperial greatness and riches. It was the cockpit in which the empires of the East and West fought for mastery. The conception of an armageddon grew naturally out of Palestine's experience; a final crisis in history made a fitting culmination to a history which consisted of a succession of crises. It would be too much to say that political crises produced true prophecy, but it may justifiably be maintained that true prophecy used them, and was perhaps even roused by them. The message of the Prophets was 'Repent for the judgment of God is at hand'; and they used the historic crises in their respective times to substantiate it. They brought into relation—a relation of cause and effect—the spiritual and moral shortcomings of the people and the threat, or fact, of invasion by a mighty power.

This relation gave them a criterion for discriminating between true and false prophecy. He who in such a situation failed to 'declare unto Jacob his transgression and unto Israel his sin' (Micah 3: 8) or proclaimed 'Peace, peace' (all is well), was a false prophet (Jeremiah 6: 14; 8: 11, Ezekiel 13: 16). The objective test for prophecy, laid down in this way by the Prophets, has a permanent significance for religion. The 'false' prophets, who claimed to be inspired; may even have shown, and probably did, the physical effects which were, in popular belief, both the product and evidence of 'inspiration'. The immoral character and behaviour of some of them refuted their claim (Jeremiah 23: 11, Ezekiel 13: 17). But none who prophesied 'smooth things' in an evil moral situation could have been inspired; those who did were all false prophets, following only the promptings of their own inclinations. Their prophecies were wishful thinking, 'from their hearts'. (Jeremiah 14: 14, Ezekiel 13: 2). God did not send them (Jeremiah 23: 11).

With their uncompromising belief in the universal and absolute sovereignty of God, the true Prophets ascribed to the false prophets a purpose in the divine scheme (Jeremiah 27: 15, Ezekiel 14: 3). But the blame for the falsehood lay on themselves. They should have known that what they said could not be true. Moral corruption must lead to destruction; that corollary follows from the belief that the world is ruled by a righteous God. If one who ignores the moral situation claims to be inspired, the claim must be false. He cannot be inspired if what he says is not true. It is not enough to say that the Prophets who left us their writings called those prophets false who disagreed with them; they had a deeper reason—their conception of God and His rule. Their thought begins with the fundamental and all-comprehensive belief that God, who is righteous, rules the universe and human history. The future must be seen by the light of His righteousness. Those who see a different future cannot be His prophets; their teachings cannot be true. In this way the Prophets implied a rational test for prophecy. It is stated explicitly in a later Rabbinic saying 'Truth is God's seal', that is, the proof of His revelation.

It is difficult to assess the measure of the Prophets' influence in their own time. They complain that their message was met by spiritual incomprehension. 'And he said, Go and tell this people. Hear ye indeed, but understand not and see ye indeed but perceive not. Make the heart of this people fat, and make their ears heavy, and shut their eyes' (Isaiah 6: 9). The Prophet either realised at the outset of his ministry that he undertook a hopeless mission, or put into the literary account of his call his later feeling of frustration. The experience was one which several Prophets report. Spiritual obtuseness prevented comprehension of their message. They could not make the people realise the spiritual and moral corruption, or inadequacy, which degraded them individually and rotted the life of the nation. Jeremiah was imprisoned and brought near to death because of his political views, and for a similar reason Amos was ordered to leave Bethel; but according to the Prophets' reports, their specifically religious teaching went uncomprehended. 'And all vision is become unto you as the words of a book that is sealed, which men deliver to one that is learned, saying, Read this, I pray thee and he saith, I cannot, for it is sealed: and the book is delivered to him that is not learned, saying, Read this, I pray thee; and he saith, I am not learned' (Isaiah 29: 11-12). And Ezekiel complained that those who came to hear him did so for pleasure, not for instruction which they intended to follow,—

frequently the fate of a popular preacher. 'And as for thee, son of man, the children of thy people talk of thee by the walls and in the doors of the houses, and speak to one another, every one to his brother, saying, Come, I pray you, and hear what is the word that cometh forth from the Lord . . . . And lo, thou art unto them as a very lovely song of one that hath a pleasant voice, and can play well on an instrument; for they hear thy words but they do them not' (Ezekiel 33: 30-32).

But the Prophets' complaint, that their instruction was unheeded, may mean no more than that the response fell far short of their eager, urgent, passionate pleading. They may have achieved much, though not all they strove for. The theocratic idea must have given them some influence, and there is specific evidence of it. One, who apparently was a leader of the community in Babylon, wrote to the high priest in Jerusalem complaining against Jeremiah's letter to the exiles, and urging that he be stopped and imprisoned (Jeremiah 29: 24-32). When they preached to kings and princes, as well as to the people, the Prophets evoked a response in which, generally, fear and indifference were mixed in varying proportions. The indifference was the usual attitude of 'those who sit at ease' to the preachers of reform. The fear, on the other hand, must have been due to the influence which the Prophets exercised over the people, for the people of Jerusalem undoubtedly often welcomed the prophets whom their rulers killed. Jeremiah would not have been imprisoned, or Amos driven from Bethel, if there was no danger that they might influence the people. Some of the things the Prophets said which disturbed the rulers must have received considerable popular approval.

Their enduring influence far exceeded the contemporary effect of their teaching. Under the impulsion of an overpowering experience of God, they strove to make men recognise His sovereignty and to live accordingly, interpreting His will and purpose for human life and human history. Their experience imposed on them a mediating function between God and men. It may have included praying to God for the people (Jeremiah 7: 16); but they themselves put almost exclusive emphasis on their duty to bring to men the instruction of God. This entailed an examination of the ways of men with a moral judgment on them (Jeremiah 6: 27). Crises in the history of their people, which emerged in the conflicts of imperial powers and involved the whole of the world which the Prophets knew, gave them the occasion for their message, and evoked it, calling for repentance to overcome the threatening consequences of unrighteousness. The crises passed, the judgment fell, but the repentance, if it came, did not last (Jeremiah 8: 20, Hosea 6: 4). But the influence of the Prophets was preserved in Judaism to serve the ultimate consummation of humanity's destiny in the Kingdom of God.

THREE

THE CONCEPTION OF GOD

THOUGH the Prophets were not theologians, a well-defined conception of God underlies their teachings and informs all their thought. One Prophet may stress one divine attribute, and another Prophet put his chief emphasis on another, but they all had the same conception of God. It was their fundamental and far-reaching contribution to the development of Judaism, and, through it, to the religious thought in the large part of the world which came under the influence of Christianity and Islam.

They discovered the One God. They were the pioneers of monotheism. They made Judaism a religion of monotheism, the only religion of monotheism in the ancient world. Before their time, the religion of the Hebrews was monolatrous or henotheistic. It demanded the exclusive worship of Jahveh their god, while recognising the existence of other—chiefly national—gods. Amos, the first of the writing Prophets, declared that Jahveh was not the national God of the Hebrews, but the God of all the nations, with the Hebrews in a special relation to Him. He does not state categorically that there is only one God, but implies it clearly. The Prophets rarely made abstract statements, they proclaimed judgments on concrete situations. So Amos declares that Jahveh will punish not only Israel but also the surrounding nations for their misdeeds. Moreover, the Prophet ascribes to the God in whose name he spoke the rule over all nations (Amos 9: 7).

Could he then have also believed in the existence of other gods? If he did, he would have put them under the God of all, so that they would have detracted from His monotheism no more than the belief in angels. But the whole tenor of his teaching excludes any kind of polytheism; and his specific prophecies against the nations refute the former belief that every nation had its own god. His monotheism is underlined by his references to Jahveh's rule over nature. 'Seek him that maketh the Pleiades and Orion, and turneth the shadow of death into the morning, and maketh the day dark with night; that calleth for the waters of the sea, and poureth them out upon the face of the earth; the Lord is his name' (Amos 5: 8). If this verse is a later interpolation, then it would at least prove that its author saw in Amos' God the God of the universe. Micah 4: 5 does not necessarily imply a belief in the existence of many gods. It probably means that though the other peoples worship other gods, the Jews will worship the true God to bring fulfilment of the preceding prophecy, that all the nations will come to worship Him. In the books of the Prophets generally, their God is the one living God, the Creator and Ruler of the whole universe; there are no other gods. The idea was revolutionary.

Monotheism emerged from the Hebrews' national religion by the mystery of God's grace. He revealed Himself first as Jahveh, the God of a particular people. It remains a mystery, to be explained only by revelation, that the belief in One God with universal sovereignty emerged clearly and emphatically from one of the many national religions of antiquity. Incidentally, it dictates a belief in the progressive revelation of God, and attests the evolutionary process in religion, that monotheism was the result of a development; the Prophets had been prepared for it by the preceding religious development of the Hebrews.

Their monotheism was not a theological abstraction, not an article of a formal creed. It was a living part of their experience. All their thought flowed from it and was dominated by it. It changed the nature of the universe and it demanded a change in the nature of man. It made the universe theocentric, centred in God so that His life filled it. That life is sometimes called power, sometimes called creation, and sometimes called sovereignty or rule. But whatever it is called, it names the activity of God's being in the universe of phenomena. It does more than that, it brings sense into all the phenomena. Problems that have exercised the philosophers of theism, the Prophets seem to ignore. The problems are real, weighing down on theistic thought with an inescapable challenge, like the problem of evil. But the Prophets did not see them because they looked at the universe and human life from God's point of view. They did not judge according to men's interests, but according to God's will. What men call evil, because it entails suffering or hardship for them, cannot be intrinsically evil since it comes in a universe created and ruled by God who is good—it belong to His scheme or order for the world. The Prophets thus judged phenomena deductively; they did not formulate inductively a conception of God's rule of the universe, but accepted as justified all that constituted the life of the universe. Their attitude followed inevitably from their theocentrism.

It led, therefore, to a kind of theistic realism. The sovereignty of God was comprehensive, so that every detail in the universal order was attributed to, or included in, His activity. That realism brought some harsh elements into their specific statements about that activity. The punishments which they say He will inflict on the nations that violate His law are sometimes—often—extremely severe; so severe that they have been quoted to support the thesis that the God of the Old Testament is a cruel God. Superficially, the argument is cogent. When the thought of the Prophets is examined more deeply, most, if not all of the cogency is eliminated in the process, or refuted in the result. The 'punishments' describe what actually happened.

The terrible experiences which it is said God will bring on the people for their sins are primarily projections into the future of what was happening in the Prophets' world. There was constant war between nations. Small peoples raided neighbouring lands for booty, empires contended for dominion over many lands to enrich themselves by tribute. In these wars, conquered peoples suffered a terrible fate. That was not infrequently the lot of the Hebrews.

The Prophets' threats of terrible 'punishments' may be partly explained by their bitter disappointment. They were human. Their exhortations went unheeded, their instructions were scorned. Driven by an overpowering sense of moral urgency, they were reduced to frustration by the spiritual and moral insensitiveness of those whom they tried to rouse. Two contrasts oppressed them, the contrast in the first place between the God of their experience and the ugliness of the world, and the related contrast between their religious zeal and the people's spiritual complacency. From both contrasts, which, to them, were the same, they suffered intense spiritual pain, as some of them testify. The grim bitterness of their prognostications was the cry of a love, which had been pained by the resistance that thwarted its eager, passionate efforts, to save its object from an impending calamity. But there is a deeper reason for their threats of severe punishments. The Prophets could not exclude terrible events from the domain of God. Their passionate conviction of His absolute and universal sovereignty precluded any way of escape. But men bring these terrible experiences on themselves. God is pained by them. He loves Israel as a father his child, or a husband his wife. When Israel suffers, He suffers. He would not deliberately cause affliction. But He rules the human world by a moral law, which emanates from His love, to promote men's well-being.

God rules the universe according to law. That idea is not explicitly stated but clearly implied in the belief, explicit or implied, that God does not change. What can that mean? It cannot mean that His decisions, fiats of His will, are unalterable? If that was the Prophets' meaning, then there would have been no sense in their exhortations to repentance with the argument that by it the people could, and would, escape from the calamities which threatened them as a punishment for their sins. God's decisions, then, can be changed. That belief can be harmonised with the idea that God does not change by conceiving His activity in terms of law. It is activity in, and through, a moral order in the universe. In that order, sin must bring its disastrous consequences, but repentance can prevent them. While the Prophets predicted calamity, they, therefore, appealed for repentance.

Another factor has to be taken into account in analysing the Prophets' conception of God for an understanding of the sternness they ascribe to Him. Physical nature is under His rule; it manifests His activity. It has a harsh aspect. A conception of God which ignores it can sentimentalise about Him. The Prophets did not ignore it. God's activity covers the whole universe, every detail in it. It maintains the order in the physical universe. 'Lift up your eyes on high, and see who hath created these that bringeth out their host by number: he calleth them all by name; by the greatness of his might, and for that he is strong in power, not one is lacking' (Isaiah 40: 26) His activity in the universe is according to law. Every event has its cause. 'Shall two walk together, except they have agreed? Will a lion roar in the forest, when he hath no prey? Will a young lion cry out of his den, if he hath taken nothing? Can a bird fall in a snare upon the earth, when no gin is set for him? Shall a snare spring up from the ground, and have taken nothing at all? Shall the trumpet be blown in the city, and the people not be afraid? shall evil befall a city, and the Lord hath not done it?' (Amos 3: 3-6). Since God and the world cannot be separated, the forces and ways of the physical world must be conceived as His activity, and the knowledge of the universe must be fitted into the conception of God. If 'incarnation' means the utmost manifestation of God in a physical embodiment, then it would be fair to say that for the Prophets the whole universe was such an incarnation.

The moral order of the universe, which conforms to God's nature, is informed, or infused, with justice and love. Though one or the other may not be evident in some particular event, both are present in the totality of the divine government of the world. The severity of the 'punishments' that sin attracts may conceal the element of love, and the assurance of love in the divine forgiveness, which not only meets repentance but pleads for it, may conceal the strictness of the justice;

but they are interwoven and harmonised in the rule of law. That is for the Prophets a fact of faith. Justice and love are integrated in their conception of God. Together they constitute the righteousness of God and the consequent righteousness in the moral order of the universe.

This combination explains God's attitude towards Israel. He loves Israel, yet threatens it with dire penalties for its transgressions. The seeming ambivalence stands out most prominently in Jeremiah. It describes the Prophet's attitude to his people; but transferred to God, it holds an essential place in the Prophet's conception of God, which is shared also by other Prophets. The Prophets' sympathy for all nations was also ascribed to God (Isaiah 21). His attitude towards all nations includes justice and love; they, too, come under His rule in the moral order of the universe.[1]

In view of the frequent stress on the sternness of the God of the Old Testament, it may be necessary, or useful, to adduce evidence of the emphasis which the Prophets put on God's love in their conception of Him. First, they affirm explicitly that He is a God of love. The relevant passages are too numerous to quote. Most of them refer to His love for Israel. The limitation, which is natural in the general context of the Prophets' thought, does not detract from the idea that He is a loving God. Moreover, there are general statements about His love which recall Exodus 34: 6f. 'He who shows mercy unto thousands' (Jeremiah 32: 18), 'Rend your heart, and not your garments, and turn unto the Lord your God; for he is gracious and full of compassion, slow to anger, and plenteous in mercy, and repenteth him of evil' (Joel 2: 13). Secondly, the Prophets imply that God is loving in their exhorta-

[1] See pages 148f.

tions to repentance. The author of Isaiah 55 sums up their doctrine for the relation between God and individuals. 'Let the wicked forsake his way, and the unrighteous man his thoughts, and let him return unto the Lord, and he will have mercy upon him; and to our God, for he will abundantly pardon' (Isaiah 55: 7). It is the Prophet's function to warn people of the consequences of sin that they may repent. (Amos 3: 3ff, Ezekiel 3: 17 and 33: 7). The doctrine that God is loving informs all the appeals of the Prophets to their own people to reform their national life. All that happens serves God's purpose to confer on men what is good (Jeremiah 29: 11). The allegory in the Book of Jonah affirms that God's love extends to all peoples (and animals). So does Isaiah 19: 24f. 'In that day shall Israel be the third with Egypt and with Assyria, a blessing in the midst of the earth: for that the Lord of hosts hath blessed them, saying, Blessed be Egypt my people, and Assyria the work of my hands, and Israel mine inheritance.'

The love of God, cannot, however, be merely sentimental affection. It serves the good, not the wishes (which may be mistaken) of its object. The rule of God is informed by that purpose. Hence it can bring dire consequences on those who violate it. Not because God lacks love: on the contrary, He grieves when men suffer, though they have brought the suffering on themselves. 'How shall I give thee up, Ephraim? how shall I deliver thee, Israel? . . . . Mine heart is turned within me, my compassions are kindled together' (Hosea 11: 8). 'Is Ephraim my dear son? is he a pleasant child? for as often as I speak against him, I do earnestly remember him still: therefore my heart is troubled for him: I will surely have mercy upon him, saith the Lord' (Jeremiah 31: 20). When Baruch,

Jeremiah's amanuensis, complained of grief and pain, the Prophet answered him: What is your sorrow compared to the agony which God feels over the impending doom. 'Thus saith the Lord, the God of Israel, unto thee, O Baruch, Thou didst say, Woe is me now! for the Lord hath added sorrow to my pain: I am weary with my groaning and I find no rest. Thus shalt thou say unto him, Thus saith the Lord: Behold, that which I have built will I break down, and that which I have planted I will pluck up': (Jeremiah 45: 2-4).

Two verses with uncertain texts call for attention in this context. It is suggested that Ezekiel 6: 9 should be emended—because the present text is grammatically impossible—so as to mean that by their disloyalty to God the people broke His heart. The traditional version of the Hebrew text of Isaiah 63: 9 says: In all their (the people's) afflictions he (God) was afflicted'. Whatever may have been the original text, or meaning, of this verse, it is significant that the form given it by a tradition, which was most probably very old, ascribes to God suffering in sympathy with the suffering of men. The idea fits the thought of the Prophets. God grieves that men sin and bring on themselves the suffering which is its consequence.

In spite of their objection to anthropomorphism, the Prophets could ascribe feeling to God without derogating from His divinity. It did not suggest to them any shortcoming in Him, or imply a human quality, that He could suffer, His love involves the possibility of suffering: as the love, so the suffering, transcends any human category. God suffers, though not like men, just as He loves with a more than human love.

The Prophets could impute sternness to God without detracting from His love, because they themselves felt both love and sternness towards their people. God's severity springs from love; love cannot be silent when its object is in danger. God pleads for the repentance that will transform a desperate situation. The Prophets felt a terrible urgency. Doom threatened. God was eager to save, but He could not ignore violations of the moral law. He works in human life according to the law of His nature, which combines harmoniously love and justice. The anger evoked by violations of His law is the anger of love that has been thwarted, and a love eager to save. It is a love that has to work through justice; without justice love is but soft sentiment, looking more to its own satisfaction than to the good of its object. God reveals His law that men may live by it; when it is violated, not only is His sovereignty offended, but His love is pained. The love cannot overlook or wipe out the offence. That would not be the way of love, it would not accord with the moral order. But the love in that order leaves open, through repentance, a way of escape from the consequences of actions that violate it. The main point to explain the severity which the Prophets ascribe to God is that, in their conception of Him, He is a God of law, and His law, in the totality of its working, manifests both His love and His justice.

Can God, whose activity is conceived in terms of law, be described as personal? The question cannot be answered with a simple Yes or No. It is complicated by the ambiguity, or complexity, in the connotation of personal, and by a seeming paradox in the Prophets' conception of God. On the one hand, they say that He thinks, wills and feels; on the other hand, they insist that He is not like man, not only because He is 'not flesh and blood', but also because He 'does not change'. When trying to penetrate into the Prophets' conception of God, we have to remember that the words 'person' and 'personality' were not in their vocabulary. That fact is important because language not only expresses thought but sets its universe of discourse; thoughts are formulated by the available words. The Prophets did not think of God as a person, but as a Power with consciousness seemingly like that of a person, but infinitely richer. He thinks, feels, judges and wills. The fact that it is difficult, or even impossible, for us to conceive such a Power without personalisation must be attributed to our human limitations. The Prophets transcended them. We may accept as a fair description of their view Robertson Smith's description of the general Biblical view: 'It was as a living personal force, not as a metaphysical entity, that Jehovah was adored by Israel',[1] if we stress the 'force'—as a personal force but more, much more, than a person. That was how the Prophets experienced God—a compelling moral force, a power pressing on their spirit. The God whom they could not see or describe was an intensely living God, burning with life, with dynamic life; constantly active, supremely conscious, and perfectly righteous, transcending, in His power, consciousness and perfection, all limitations, including the limitations of personality. The essence of God's being cannot be like the essence of human being. He is both other than man and wholly different from man, so that He cannot be defined in His essential nature by any terms which can be applied to man. Man's essence is personality, God's essence is divinity.

The Prophets, therefore, avoided anthropomorphisms. Ezekiel may present an exception. In his first vision, he sees a 'form like that of a man' seated on the heavenly throne of glory. It is tempting to seek a way, and not difficult to find one, which would explain away

[1] W. R. Smith: *The Prophets*, p. 63.

this crude anthropomorphism especially as in the rest of his book, Ezekiel seems deliberately to avoid all anthropomorphisms in the descriptions of his visions of God (Note 3: 23 and 10: 1). But if the text must be taken literally, he must be treated as an exception: the Prophets generally did not have an anthropomorphic conception of God, in spite of the anthropomorphic language they use in describing His activity and self-consciousness. They say, however, nothing positive about the essence of God, except to insist on His otherness from man. In spite of the early stories in the Bible, Judaism developed early in its history a strong objection to ascribing any physical form to God. So the author of Deuteronomy 4, in recounting the story of Sinai, stresses that the people 'saw no manner of form but only heard a voice', obviously to express what Jewish philosophers later called the incorporeality of God. In the Priestly code in the Pentateuch, old stories were re-written to avoid anthropomorphic statements about God. The Prophets objected not only to crude anthropomorphism in the description of God and His activity, but also to any correspondence in essence between Him and man. Men can 'imitate' God by ethical striving, but God and man are essentially different.

I am inclined to think that there had long been a current of thought in the religion of the Hebrews which tried to transcend all human categories in the conception of God. One ground for that view is the story in Exodus 3. When Moses asked God to define Himself, he received an answer which has puzzled scholars but apparently did not puzzle the author of the story. The answer is translated in the English versions 'I am that I am' or 'I will be that I will be'. The Hebrew root word means 'to be' or 'to become'. It is conceivable that the writer may have intended to define God as 'Being'. Biblical Hebrew lacks abstracts, so that abstract ideas had to be expressed by circumlocutions. But even if this conjecture be rejected, the fact remains that the author avoided any definition of God beyond affirming, in some way, His being. And it may justify the assertion that from an early stage in its development Judaism harboured a tendency to avoid human categories in the conception of God, which came fully to the surface in the thought of the Prophets. They had a supra-personal conception of God. They combined it, however, with language about Him taken from human consciousness. They could use no other language to describe His activity. Divinity acts like human personality; not on a personal but on a divine plane. The distinction is important; it makes the conception of God intellectually tenable for those who want His being to be commensurate with infinity by transcending all limitations such as those which circumscribe human personality. At the same time, God is not a mere abstraction but a living reality who responds to man's emotional need for a Friend in the universe.

This conception of God has, furthermore, the theological merit that it eases the combination of divine transcendence and immanence. The Power that transcends the universe works in it; so that a Prophet can affirm that God, who is supremely sublime, is very near to those who turn to Him in their need (Isaiah 57: 15). The idea of divine transcendence may also be present as an adumbration in the term, applied to God in the first part of the Book of Isaiah, the Holy One of Israel. Holiness describes the ethical perfection of God but also His sublime essence. The first is in His immanent activity; the second, in His transcendent being.

FOUR

THE MORAL LAW

The Prophets constantly refer to 'the law of God'. It is binding on men and nations. What did they mean by it? To find the answer we have to go back to its Hebrew original. The Hebrew word translated 'law' is *torah,* which means literally instruction. The Septuagint translates it by *nomos,* law, following the later development in Judaism which gave the law in the Pentateuch the paramount place in the Scripture. In Jewish usage *torah* never lost completely its larger meaning. It has been, and still is, often applied to the whole body of Scripture, which includes Bible and Talmud. The Prophets use it in its original sense. The *torah* of God is instruction from God. It, therefore, includes not only injunctions for right conduct but also the truths about God Himself and His activity. It covers all that the Prophets meant by the knowledge which comes from God. The 'law of God' is, therefore, used by them in the general sense of divine revelation.

Like the English 'revelation', the Hebrew *torah* is both an abstract and concrete noun. It describes the way by which God's mind and will are made known to men, and the ideas and forms of conduct He requires. So, the Prophets called their teaching 'the law of God'. 'Hear the word of the Lord, ye rulers of Sodom; give ear unto the law of our God, ye people of Gomorrah' (Isaiah 1 : 10). Not to heed the Prophets' exhortations or advice was to reject the law of God. When Isaiah, frustrated and depressed by the stony indifference to his ministry, asks his disciples to preserve 'the law', he means his sermons, the instruction he has brought from God. 'To the law and to the testimony! If they speak not according to this word, surely there is no morning for them' (Isaiah 8: 20, cf. 5: 24, 8: 6-8, 30: 12-14). When the King and his advisers do not consult him about a political policy, he accuses them of trying to hide their plan from God (Isaiah 29: 15). The other Prophets, too, call their teaching, equating it with the teaching of all the prophets, the law of God. 'And thou shalt say unto them, Thus saith the Lord: If ye will not hearken to me, to walk in my law, which I have set before you, to hearken to the words of my servants the prophets, whom I send unto you, even rising up early and sending them, but ye have not hearkened'. (Jeremiah 26: 4-5). 'Yea, they made their hearts as an adamant stone lest they should hear the law, and the words which the Lord of hosts had sent by his spirit by the hand of the former prophets' (Zechariah 7: 12). It is one of the evils—perhaps the greatest in an evil time—that the prophets are silent. They have no message from God for the people. 'The law is slacked' (Habakkuk 1: 4).

The priests also claimed to give instruction from God; and some of the Prophets refer with respect to 'the law of the priests'. 'For the priest's lips should keep knowledge, and they should seek the law at his mouth; for he is the messenger of the Lord of hosts' (Malachi 2: 7). Ezekiel puts the 'law of the priests' with the 'counsel of the elders' and the 'vision of the prophets' as the channels of God's guidance (Ezekiel 7: 26). The priest's law was a recognised institution of religion, so much so that the people could not believe that it would come to an end (Jeremiah 18: 18). Jeremiah's prophecy of the destruction of the Temple could not be true. Religion could not perish; its institutions are indestructible. But, Jeremiah insisted, institutions cannot preserve religion. Without faith they are powerless.

From all the references to the 'law of the priests' two inferences may be fairly drawn. First, it dealt largely, if not exclusively, with ritual prescriptions (Haggai 2: 11ff). Its character, therefore, did not commend it to those Prophets who saw in ritualism a spiritual stumbling block, a hindrance to true religion. Secondly, it was a literal tradition transmitted either orally or in a book. Its literalism aggravated its danger to true religion, its harm to the spirit. So, Prophets condemned it. 'How do ye say, We are wise, and the law of the Lord is with us? But behold, the false pen of the scribes hath wrought falsely' (Jeremiah 8: 8). The priest's instruction could not produce the religious attitude (Isaiah 29: 13). Book religion, or memorised religious formulae, could not give the instruction of God. That could be apprehended only by the heart through its faith.

The law of God was, for the Prophets, not a book. They do not refer to any book in support of their exhortations. Malachi, the latest of the prophetic books, concludes with an appeal to 'remember the law of Moses'. But the other Prophets do not mention such a law. When they mention Moses, he is not referred to as a lawgiver (Hosea 12: 14, Jeremiah 15: 1). It appears, therefore, that before Malachi there was no 'law of Moses' with authority for religious thought and practice. The conclusion is supported by several other facts. The historic and literary study of the Pentateuch has established beyond doubt that it could not in its entirety be the law of Moses. Isaiah, Hosea, Jeremiah and others could not have scoffed at sacrifices if they had known of laws about sacrifices coming from Moses. Nor would Ezekiel have diverged from Leviticus in his prescriptions for the sacrificial system if the laws in Leviticus existed in his time with Mosaic authority.

One more point deserves mention in this context. When Jeremiah used the Rechabites' refusal to drink wine as a text for a sermon on religious loyalty, he said to the assembly that had gathered to witness the scene: See how loyal these Rechabites are to the instruction given them by their ancestor Jonadab. Surely he would have naturally continued: But see how disloyal you are to the instruction of your ancestor Moses, if Moses was recognised at the time as the great lawgiver. What Jeremiah did say was: 'But I (God) have spoken to you, rising up early and speaking (through the prophets); and ye have not hearkened unto me' (Jeremiah 35: 14-15). Silence permits no certain conclusion, but the Prophets' persistent silence about Moses would be most surprising if he had, in their time, stood out as the supreme lawgiver.

Jeremiah's attitude to Deuteronomy does not weaken, much less refute, this conclusion, and may even strengthen it. He does not, unfortunately, state it clearly; it has to be inferred, with the uncertainty that must attend inference from ambiguity. Early in his ministry a book was found in the Temple, which, scholars agree, was probably the main part of the present book of Deuteronomy. On the basis of it, King Josiah instituted far-reaching religious reforms, which are reported in the twenty-second and twenty-third chapters of the Second Book of Kings. What was Jeremiah's attitude to the book and the consequent reformation? The two passages in his book which might be taken as references to it present opposing views. At any rate, on the surface. In Chapter 8 he condemns reliance on a written law; it is the work of false scribes (verse 8). In Chapter 11 he says that he received instruction from God to proclaim 'the words of this covenant' (verses 2 and 6). If both passages refer to Deuteronomy, they can be reconciled by assuming that the Prophet's attitude underwent a change, that he welcomed it at first in the belief that it marked a real revival of true religion, but, disappointed in the event, he blamed the book for the self-satisfied formalism which it engendered. The sequence of the two passages has no significance; the book of Jeremiah has been disarranged in transmission. It is, however, hard to reconcile the suggestion that the Prophet at any time approved a book which commands sacrifices, though in a simpler form than the priestly code, with his specific declaration (Chapter 7, verse 22) that God did not command sacrifices. These two passages may be reconciled in another way; it might be reasonably conjectured that Jeremiah was impressed only by the act of re-dedication (II. Kings 23: 3), which inaugurated Josiah's reformation. By either assumption, the Prophet distinguished the covenant from the book. The covenant was the re-dedication. It signified a solemn and earnest declaration of loyalty to God.

'Covenant' has two meanings, one abstract, the other concrete. It may mean a contractual relation or the document of a contract. The distinction is brought out clearly by a later Prophet. 'As for me, this is my covenant with them, saith the Lord: My spirit that is upon thee, and my words which I have put in thy mouth, shall not depart out of thy mouth nor out of the mouth of thy seed, nor out of the mouth of thy seed's seed, saith the Lord, from henceforth and for ever' (Isaiah 59: 21). 'Covenant' describes the relation between God and Israel which is a matter of the spirit, a spiritual bond, like the bond between husband and wife, established by the election which God conferred on Israel in His grace.

The law of God, His revelation, lays down its terms, what it specifically imposes; it is the deed of the contract. To disobey it violates the covenant, breaks the relation with God. Because the covenant and the law are thus inseparably united, they can be used interchangeably, but they do not have the same specific significance. The covenant relation is expressed in, and maintained, by, the law. In the ultimate fulfilment of God's purpose, it will be established in such a way that the law will be spontaneously fulfilled. This is the meaning of Jeremiah's prophecy of the new covenant. 'Behold, the days come, saith the Lord, that I will make a new covenant with the house of Israel, and with the house of Judah, not according to the covenant that I made with their fathers in the day that I took them by the hand to bring them out of the land of Egypt; which my covenant they brake, although I was an husband unto them, saith the Lord. But this is the covenant that I will make with the house of Israel after those days, saith the Lord; I will put my law in their inward parts, and in their hearts will I write it, and I will be their God, and they shall be my people' (Jeremiah 31: 31-34).

The last verse opens a clear view into the Prophet's mind. He did not mean that the law will be changed. He could not have meant that; he argues again and again that God has constantly revealed His law through prophets. It does not change just as He does not change. God's law is eternal; there cannot be an old one to abrogate or a new one to promulgate. Jeremiah must have meant that this eternal law will ultimately receive spontaneous obedience from men, when they will be radically changed. Originally, when the covenant relation was established, its requirements were written on tablets of stone; in the time to come they will be written on different material. They will be the same, but inscribed in the hearts of men. The new heart and new spirit, cleansed from sinfulness, will harbour fully that inner sense of relation with God, which is the knowledge of Him and compels obedience to His law. 'And I will give them an heart to know me, that I am the Lord, and they shall be my people, and I will be their God; for they shall return unto me with their whole heart' (Jeremiah 24: 7). Ezekiel's prophecy about the new heart and the new spirit, repeated several times, may mean the same thing as Jeremiah's prophecy of the new covenant.

What, then, was the law which belonged to the covenant? Jeremiah's reference to the law written on stone suggests that the answer should be the Decalogue. But his whole book gives a more comprehensive conception of it. It is the spiritual and moral instruction in revelation. The revelation which was given to the Prophets individually conveyed it, but it was not their possession. It had objective reality. When a Prophet complained of indifference to the law of God, he often meant refusal to heed what he said, to follow his advice, or to adopt the reforms he urged, but he also meant that this indifference violated the moral and spiritual order of the universe. The 'law of God' is not his words but the reality behind them (Amos 2: 4). It consists of the truth and righteousness which live in God. The revelation emanating from Him remains in Him. The Prophets' instruction from God was a report about Him. He reveals Himself in His law. The truth and righteousness which the Prophets taught they learnt in their experience of Him.

This aspect of the Prophets' thought must be stressed for an understanding of the complex ideas covered by their references to 'the law of God'. By revelation God gives men instruction in the knowledge of Himself. They can know Him only by the light which He sheds on them, as the sun is known by the light it radiates. But in revealing Himself, He teaches men the way they should live to conform with His nature and His rule. When, therefore, the Prophets call their pronouncements 'the law of God', they claim for them objective validity. The law transcends the lives of the Prophets. 'Your fathers, where are they? and the prophets, do they live for ever?' (Zechariah 1: 5). The law of God exists apart from men; it expresses the nature of God and belongs to His eternal essence. In later Jewish thought, the Law was given an independent existence which began before the creation of the world. That was the metaphysical way of expressing its eternity. The Prophets, who did not think metaphysically, expressed its eternal quality by conceiving it as a revelation which is perennial and ever the same, being the expression of the living, constantly active, God. It is an integral part of His rule of the universe, in which He reveals Himself.

The law of God is, therefore universal. Revealed to Israel, it was intended for all men. So the author of the poems about the Suffering Servant of God could say that the nations wait for His law (teaching); and the books of Isaiah and Micah incorporate a prophecy that 'in the end of days' all nations will flow to 'the mountain of the Lord's house', to receive His law. Later apocalyptic, which is the continuation of prophecy informed by the spirit of the Prophets though lacking their vigour, looks forward steadily to the acceptance by all peoples of the religion which has God's law. But the law of God is binding on all the nations before the final consummation of human history. Their several histories are under God's rule, so that they must suffer the consequences of their failure to recognise Him and to obey His moral demands. After all, they could see the futility of their idols, and learn from their national experiences about the moral government of the universe.

When the Prophets speak of 'the law of God', they refer mostly to its moral requirements. Morality is an integral part of the knowledge of God. The moral law belongs to His revelation. The moral principles, which men must follow, are the attributes of God which He manifests in His rule of the universe, so that morality belongs to, and has its basis in, the universal order. The commandments in the law are not the arbitrary edicts of a haughty sovereign who wants to impose his will on his subjects. They issue from God's nature, expressing His love and justice. The law, therefore, serves men's good.

The fact that morality prescribes ways which promote human welfare does not refute its divine origin; but rather proves it. The revelation of the law comes in God's loving activity towards men. Plato's question whether a law is good because God gave it or God gave it because it is good can have no logical relevance to the Prophets' thought. The alternatives say the same thing. Goodness inheres in God's moral order; what is good comes from Him, so that to say that a law comes from Him is to say that it is good, and to say that a law is good is to say that it comes from Him. The 'because' in the alternatives posed in Plato's question contains a logical fallacy; it suggests a causal relation where there is identity. Of course morality serves men's good; for it emanates from God who is concerned for men's well-being. Its pragmatic value does not prove that men have evolved it but that it accords with the nature of God.

Though the moral law expresses God, it suits the nature of man. The Prophets would have agreed with the author of Deuteronomy 30: 11-14; 'For this commandment which I command thee this day, it is not too hard for thee, neither is it far off. It is not in heaven, that thou shouldest say, who shall go up for us to heaven, and bring it unto us, and make us to hear it, that we may do it? But the word is very nigh unto thee, in thy mouth, and in thy heart, that thou mayest do it'. Though divine, the moral law is also human. It is not an external authority but an inner force. The moral sense is in the endowment conferred on men by God, which, when fully exercised, gives divine significance, and therefore real value to their lives. God has implanted it in men just as he implanted in them a knowledge of the laws of nature. After describing the process which the farmer follows in tilling the soil, Isaiah concludes 'This (the farmer's knowledge) also cometh forth from the Lord of hosts, who is wonderful in counsel, and excellent in wisdom' (Isaiah 28: 29). God has taught the farmer the laws of nature and he has sense enough to follow them. So God has implanted moral guidance in the nature of man. If men would only have sense enough to follow it! One day they will, when loyalty to God will fill them with the spirit of His commandments. They will then spontaneously obey His law; their human nature will have attained to its full spiritual maturity.

By conceiving morality as part of the law of God, the Prophets gave its requirements the status, or quality, of absolutes. Being an expression of His nature, they are eternal and unchangeable. Men may mistake the moral law, but the true prophets have always taught it. The evidence from history that men's moral standards have changed, and from sociology that they vary, would not have disturbed the Prophets' belief in an absolute morality. Men did not always 'know God'. Abraham's ancestors 'across the river' did not know Him. And even when the Hebrews had been told about Him, their stupidity prevented them from understanding what He meant to them and what He required from them. The inadequacies and failures in men's moral apprehensions prove only their folly, not God's silence. Men's judgments of right and wrong may be relative to their spiritual and moral development, but morality must consist of absolutes. That follows from the belief in a God of righteousness. Righteousness cannot mean to Him different things in different ages. Men must always follow Him as the moral pattern for their lives.

The question whether men can know the will of God did not arise for the Prophets. They were themselves the answer. Sceptics questioned their prophetic claim: 'For who hath stood in the council of the Lord, that he should perceive and hear his word? who hath marked my word, and heard it?' (Jeremiah 23: 18). The scepticism which affirms that 'we cannot know', is religion's deadliest enemy, more deadly than some doubt; it attacks religion by corrosion. Doubt has a legitimate and even useful place in religious thought. Like faith, it testifies to the grand mystery in the universe, and with faith, it can generate spiritual striving. But the belief that 'we cannot know' blocks the strivings of the spirit, and crushes the spirit itself into futility. True, men cannot know absolutes, but their limitations do not disprove the existence of the absolutes, which challenge their limited capacities to endless intellectual and moral endeavour. The striving for righteousness and the search for truth derive their value, as they draw impulsion, from the belief that human morality and knowledge represent absolute righteousness and truth, and that progress in them advances the human hold on reality and men's integration in the life of the universe.

Because the law of God expresses His attributes, to obey it establishes and maintains man's intimate relation with Him. It brings the revelation of God to men; by following it men come to God. The obedience must be spontaneous, not imposed from without but impelled from within. True, in the actual human situation, the moral law must be obeyed even where the inward impulsion is lacking. Men can in this way deliver themselves from the corruption which they have inflicted on themselves. Through the chosen and persistent pursuit of righteousness they open for themselves the way to God. The fulfilment of the moral law establishes the relation between man and God, bringing God to men and men to God. Through it, therefore, men attain to the blessing in that relation.

FIVE

ETHICAL PRINCIPLES

THE ethical principles laid down by the moral law are clearly defined by the Prophets and repeated frequently and emphatically. They are summed up in Jeremiah's statement of the *summum bonum:* 'Thus saith the Lord, let not the wise man glory in his wisdom, neither let the mighty man glory in his might, let not the rich man glory in his riches; but let him that glorieth glory in this, that he understandeth, and knoweth me, that I am the Lord who exercises loving-kindness, justice and righteousness, in the earth; for in these things I delight, saith the Lord' (Jeremiah 9: 23f). To apprehend the ethical teaching of the Prophets, the meaning must be analysed of the Hebrew words which are translated, 'loving-kindness, justice and righteousness'.

Chesed, which is translated in the quotation from Jeremiah by 'loving-kindness'—and elsewhere variously by 'kindness', 'loving-kindness' or 'mercy'—describes an attitude of God towards men, the right attitude of men towards God, and of men towards one another. No English word, or even phrase, can fully convey its meaning. When attributed to God in His attitude to, or treatment of, men, it may correspond to grace. As the attitude of men towards God, it means loving and faithful devotion and comprises all that flows from it. It has this meaning in Hosea's famous utterance that God desires *chesed* rather than sacrifices; it is paralleled in the second part of the verse, by 'the knowledge of God', which means an effective, dynamic sense of intimate relation with Him. *Chesed* has this meaning also in Jeremiah 2: 2 where God says to Israel 'I remember the *chesed* of your youth' which was like 'the faithful love of a bride'.

According to some scholars, it has the primary meaning of eager zeal. The religious zealots in the time of the Maccabees were called *Chasidim,* and the same name was given to, or appropriated by, a sect of enthusiastic Jewish pietists which arose in the 18th century in Poland. In these contexts *chesed* carried the connotation of religious zeal, enthusiastic devotion in the service of God. In Isaiah 57: 1, 'men of *chesed*' is parallel to 'the righteous'. *Chasid,* that is, one who practised *chesed,* is used extensively in the Psalms and possibly also in other parts of the Bible for one who shows utmost devotion to God. 'The *chasid* is perished out of the earth, and there is none upright among men; they all lie in wait for blood; they hunt every man his brother with a net' (Micah 7: 2).

Chesed almost corresponds to our 'piety' before limited usage and unfavourable associations had spoilt it. Like it, *chesed* meant faithful, devoted love, loving devotion, or affectionate loyalty to God. Translated into action, it requires the worship of God, in loyal love, and conduct towards men which expresses love or kindness. Personal service in charity is called in Rabbinic literature and in later Judaism, doing acts of *chesed.* Zechariah may use it in that sense (Zechariah 7: 9). Prophets may occasionally have used it with a dual meaning, to urge at the same time the right attitude to God and right conduct towards men (Hosea 4: 1, 10: 12, 12: 7, Isaiah 16: 5). It may have that dual meaning in Micah's definition of religion (Micah 6: 8). As an ethical principle, it is dynamic love deeply felt, graciously radiant, working in ways which please or benefit others. It is, in one word, the principle in the commandment 'Thou shalt love thy neighbour as thyself' (Leviticus 19: 18).

Mishpat, translated 'justice' in the quotation from Jeremiah, means, in the first place, a judgment of a court, or a decree of government, a legal decision or a law. In this sense it was ascribed to God's rule of the universe. In two cases it may mean the natural order (Isaiah 28: 26 and 40: 14). When applied to God, it is often the collective name for the laws which He, as the Ruler of the universe, has decreed for men; so that in the poems of the suffering servant in Deutero-Isaiah it is synonymous with religion. 'Behold my servant, whom I uphold; my chosen, in whom my soul delighteth; I have put my spirit upon him; he shall bring forth *mishpat* to the nations'. (Isaiah 42: 1). God's laws express His justice; so *mishpat* came to mean a just law or judgment, and then justice. It is the duty of human rulers and judges to make their judgments and laws conform to the justice of God's rule. Right judgments and right laws embody justice. In the general sense of justice it came to be applied to the relations between men. It may be that when a Prophet pleads for *mishpat* he means justice in the most inclusive sense, right decisions by judges, just laws by rulers, and, in general, fair treatment of others. This is the justice which God exercises in His rule; He requires its like in men's actions. It is consideration for the rights and needs of human beings as persons.

Tsedakah, translated 'righteousness' in the quotation from Jeremiah, was used in so many, though related, senses that it cannot be defined simply. Like *chesed* and *mishpat* it was attributed both to God and enjoined on men. It was originally a technical legal term, referring both to the verdict in a lawsuit and to the litigant or claimant in whose favour it was given. It described the verdict as just. So it sometimes has the general meaning of justice. But a verdict of 'not guilty' when an innocent man is accused, not only expresses justice, it also establishes the innocence of the accused; it 'justifies' him, clears him of guilt. The verb to which *tsedakah* is related, as its noun, seems to be used with this meaning in Isaiah 53: 11, which describes the achievement of the suffering servant. Though the text is too confused to permit an exact translation, it does warrant the general interpretation that the servant will, because of his suffering, 'justify' others, that is, remove their sin, and establish them in righteousness, not by vicarious atonement, but by his influence.

Out of its forensic origin, *tsedakah* developed a variety of meanings. In all of them it has an ethical content; whether applied to God or men it covers the whole of morality. Possibly moral excellence would come nearest to expressing its idea. 'Righteousness', when taken in this sense, translates it appropriately. In God it is moral perfection, in men it is virtue.

When applied to God, it extends, however, much further than in its application to men, to correspond with God's rule of the universe. Facts must ultimately attest that rule, so that in the consummation of history the righteousness of God will stand out clearly to justify His government. So Deutero-Isaiah uses *tsedakah* for the fulfilment of God's purpose in human history. 'I bring near my righteousness' (Isaiah 46: 13). It is synonymous with God's victory. 'Keep ye judgment, and do righteousness, for my salvation (literally, victory) is near to come, and my righteousness to be revealed' (Isaiah 56: 1). The fulfilment of God's purposes means both the triumph of righteousness, and the justification of His rule, the conclusive proof of its justice.

Within the limited human sphere, *tsedakah* is the moral essence of the good life and the moral quality in right conduct. Jeremiah uses it in that sense in his definition of the *summum bonum*. It does not occur in Micah's definition of true religion; but it is included, in its general sense, in the third element in that definition, 'to walk humbly with God', and it is covered more specifically by *mishpat* (justice) and *chesed* (loving-kindness), the two elements in the highest moral attainment in character and deeds.

Love and justice together constitute righteousness; they are not contrasting qualities. For the most part, the Prophets were concerned in their ethical teaching with the treatment of the weaker members of society by the stronger, of the poor by the rich, of humble subjects by rulers, of needy suitors by judges. The weak have the right to be treated with humane consideration. In their case justice can be given only by love. The principle applies to all human relations. When conceived strictly in personal terms, so that nothing comes into consideration but what pertains to persons, whether as rights or obligations, as dues or duties, love and justice are one. They separate into a dichotomy only when considerations of status or property break their harmony.

The duty of holiness is not specifically enjoined by the Prophets, among ethical duties. The omission may suggest that the concept of holiness had not yet attained fully its ethical content; it retained the significance of separation. In this sense, the adjective 'holy' is applied to the remnant in Isaiah 4: 3 and 6: 13, and the author of the third part of the Book of Isaiah calls the future Israel 'the holy people' (Isaiah 62: 12). It may, however, be inferred from Isaiah's, and the other Prophets', general teaching that holiness in these contexts includes moral excellence. The main stress in it is on the distinctiveness achieved by a full and clear relation with God, but that distinctiveness includes high ethical attainment. It has a related connotation when it is applied to God; it emphasises His supreme sublimity, as in Isaiah's 'the Holy One of Israel' and in Isaiah 57: 15; but God is sanctified, which may mean that He shows His holiness, through righteousness (Isaiah 5: 16). The Prophets do not urge men to strive for holiness. It is, however, implied in all their moral exhortations, and it comes to almost explicit expression in Micah's 'to walk humbly with God', and in the Prophets' emphasis on *chesed* towards God.

The Prophets define right conduct in some detail. Who lives rightly? 'He that walketh righteously, and speaketh uprightly; he that despiseth the gain of oppressions, that shaketh his hands from holding of bribes, that stoppeth his ears from hearing of blood, and shutteth his eyes from looking upon evil' (Isaiah 33: 14-15). 'Is this not the fast that I have chosen? to loose the bonds of wickedness, to undo the bands of the yoke, and to let the oppressed go free, and that ye break every yoke? Is it not to deal thy bread to the hungry, and that thou bring the poor that are cast out to thy house? when thou seest the naked, that thou cover him; and that thou hide not thyself from thine own flesh? . . . . to draw out thy soul to the hungry, and satisfy the afflicted soul' (Isaiah 58: 6, 7 and 10a).

Ezekiel defines the righteous (religious) man as one who does justice (*mishpat*) and righteousness (*tsedakah*) 'eats no flesh with blood in it'; refrains from idolatry, maintains sexual purity, 'and has not wronged any, but has restored to the debtor his pledge, has despoiled none by violence, has given his bread to the hungry, and has covered the naked with a garment; he that has not lent his money at interest, neither has taken any increase, that has withdrawn his hand from iniquity, has executed true judgment between man and man, has walked in my statutes, and has kept my judgments, to deal truly; he is righteous, he shall surely live, saith the Lord God'. (Ezekiel 18: 7-9). Zechariah defines ethical duties in a way which recalls Leviticus 19. 'Thus hath the Lord of hosts spoken, saying, Execute true judgment, and show mercy and compassion every man to his brother; and oppress not the widow, nor the fatherless, the stranger, nor the poor; and let none of you imagine evil against his brother in your heart' (Zechariah 7: 9f). In another passage the Prophet adds 'Speak ye every man the truth with his neighbour; execute the judgment of truth and peace in your gates; and love no false oath; for all these are things that I hate, saith the Lord' (Zechariah 8: 16b-17). The wrongs the Prophets condemn define further the ethical duties they enjoin on men. They condemn dishonesty and sharp practice in trade (Hosea 12: 7-8, Micah 6: 10-12, Amos 8: 4ff); taking advantage of poor farmers to make them pay oppressive rent or interest (Amos 5: 11); depriving the smallholder of his land by foreclosing on mortgages (Isaiah 5: 8, Micah 2: 1-2). They reprove kings, princes and the rich for their luxury and frivolity. They condemn sexual vices. Isaiah upbraids women for their artificial manners and ostentation (Isaiah 3: 16-24 and 32: 9-12).

The ethical principles which the Prophets enunciate are intended for the lives of individuals and human societies. Justice and love must guide both. Similarly, the ethical duties which they impose are obligations on both persons and governments. By them men and nations attain to righteousness.

SIX

THE GOOD LIFE

JEREMIAH'S definition of the *summum bonum* states the qualities of the good life.[1] It requires justice, loving-kindness and righteousness, but they must be rooted in the knowledge of God. The knowledge of God, in all the books of the Prophets, means a sense of intimate relation with Him. It obviously involves an intellectual apprehension of Him, a mental affirmation of His reality, and a right conception of Him, but its main emphasis is on trustful devotion to Him. It is faith, not in the theological sense, but in the sense of a personal relation with God. The Prophets have no word for faith in the theological sense, nor has the Hebrew Bible. The right intellectual belief in God is clearly, and even emphatically, implied in all the teaching of the Prophets, especially in their denunciations of the worship of 'strange gods'. Other gods did not exist; they are 'vanity', without reality. It is worse than folly to worship them. In their condemnation of such worship and of idolatry they had in mind both the collective religion of the nation and the personal religion of individuals. Men must individually recognise the One God, who is the true God; but it is not enough to believe in His existence. He must be trusted.

In various contexts, the Prophets urge men to have faith in God. 'Therefore turn thou to thy God; keep mercy and judgment, and wait on thy God continually'

[1] See page 69.

(Hosea 12: 6). 'Blessed is the man that trusteth in the Lord, and whose hope the Lord is' (Jeremiah 17: 7). On the day of judgment 'a man shall look unto his Maker, and his eyes will turn to the Holy One of Israel' (Isaiah 17: 7). The paramount importance of faith for the good life is stated epigrammatically by Habakkuk. The righteous lives by his faith—lives, that is, in the consciousness of relation with God, and of His favour (Habakkuk 2: 4). The righteous man is here—the Hebrew word is *tsaddik*—he who fulfils the religious requirements for the good life.

Faith means both trust in God and faithfulness to Him, reliance on God and loyalty to him. From this attitude to God, men derive the power of confidence. It means trust in Him and His rule, which keeps men steadfast in devotion to Him, and firm in their own spirit amidst all vicissitudes. Its two meanings, trust and steadfastness, are brought together in Isaiah 7: 9. The king is frightened by a threat of invasion. The Prophet advises him not to yield to the threatening powers nor to call in the aid of Assyria against them. What then? Trust in God! If you do not have faith you cannot stand firm (Isaiah 7: 9). 'Have faith' translates an active form and 'stand firm' a passive form of the same Hebrew verb. (The same play on words to emphasise the importance and power of faith in God occurs in II. Chronicles 20: 20). The faith which trusts in God held a large place in Isaiah's teaching. On another critical occasion he admonished: 'He who has faith will not get excited (inwardly disturbed)' (Isaiah 28: 16).

Like Jeremiah, Hosea gives 'the knowledge of God' the primary place in religion, and, therefore, in the good life. He equates it with *chesed,* loving devotion, towards God. 'I (God) desire *chesed* rather than sacrifices and the knowledge of God rather than burnt offerings' (Hos. 6: 6). Conceivably *chesed* might be interpreted in this verse to mean loving conduct between men; but the obvious parallelism between the two parts of the verse makes it more likely that the Prophet identified *chesed* and the knowledge of God. Both involve the attitude of faith.

The third element in Micah's definition of religion, 'to walk humbly with God', may also be intended to describe the attitude towards God, and the sense of relation with Him, which constitute the faith of personal religion. Some uncertainty attaches to the Hebrew word translated 'humbly'. It occurs in only one other place in the Bible where the uncertainty is, however, not removed by the context. In Rabbinic literature it has a meaning which would justify interpreting Micah's words to mean a simple and devout faith in God. Some scholars trace to it the name of Essenes, taken by them because of their ideal of piety, which consisted of devout faith with humility and austerity in living.

Superficially, the Prophets' conception of personal religion omits the communion with God described by the phrase: 'Alone with the Alone'. Hosea exhorts to prayer (Hosea 14: 2); but the context prevents the suggestion that he had in mind personal communion with God. The Prophets themselves, however, practised it, as is shown by their prayers and the colloquies with God which they report (Jeremiah 12, Habakkuk). It gave them the mystical experience which generated all their prophesying. It was not the emotionalism which may be roused by the performance of rites and which is sometimes mistaken for mysticism; it was the supreme awareness of God. And they clearly implied that such an experience of God is possible for all men, who will attain to it when the sin which bars the way to God is removed. 'For they shall all know me, from the least of them unto the greatest of them, saith the Lord; for I will forgive their iniquity, and their sin will I remember no more' (Jeremiah 31: 34). From their own experience they deduced the belief that all men could be filled with the 'knowledge of God'; for they considered themselves ordinary men whom God had impressed into His service by filling them and overpowering them with His inspiration. They were exceptional not in the quality of their humanity but only by exaltation to its highest spiritual potentiality. They possessed—or, it might be said, were possessed by—the knowledge of God, the consciousness of an immediate and close relation with Him, which is the ideal for all men. A story in Numbers makes Moses exclaim: Would that all the people were prophets, that the Lord might put his spirit upon them (Numbers 11: 29). All men have the capacity for the mystical experience, which they can attain if they will open themselves to God's inspiration. Mere formal worship cannot give it, it can come only through the outreaching of the whole personality towards God. And 'the knowledge of God' attained in this way, gives both the motive for, and the impulse to, living the good life.

The time will come when God will inspire all men. 'And it shall come to pass afterwards that I will pour out my spirit unto all flesh; and your sons and your daughters shall prophesy, your old men shall dream dreams, your young men shall see visions; and also upon the servants and upon the handmaids in those days will I pour out my spirit' (Joel 2: 28-29). They will all feel the guiding pressure of the divine spirit. All men can hear the voice of God if they will listen.

They do not need an intermediary. The remoteness of these hopes from actuality must not be allowed to obscure their significance; they give supreme value to personal religion. And they indicate the possibility for men to attain in it the highest, and full, realisation of their spiritual and moral kinship with God. That realisation must come. The kind of mysticism which impelled the Prophets to their mission is ultimately a spiritual necessity for all men and the moral hope of mankind. Personal religion involves it, in the varying degrees possible for individuals according to their spiritual capacities. The ideal is for all men to attain fully to the communion with God which it describes. That is the knowledge of God which exalts human life to its highest dignity, and the love (*chesed*) which God wants from men. To aim, therefore, for the mystic experience of God, pertains to the good life. And personal righteousness flows from it.

The practice of righteousness is integral in the good life. To 'know' God involves spontaneous obedience to His law. Therefore Jeremiah declared that when men's relation with God is perfectly established, they will have His law in their hearts. Ezekiel prophesies that they will then have 'a new heart and a new spirit'; and Isaiah promises that after the people have been purged by suffering, they will behold God, their Teacher and hear His voice guiding them. Deutero-Isaiah prophesied to Jerusalem: 'All thy children shall be taught of the Lord'. All these prophecies can refer only to the spiritual attainment of individuals. The people will, individually, be filled with the powerful sense of relation with God, which will impel them to the practice of righteousness.

The importance which the Prophets give to the personal relation with God has perhaps been obscured by their emphasis on right conduct, which might suggest a lack of interest in the spiritual as distinct from the ethical aspect of religion. The inference would be mistaken. In the first place, they conceived morality as a spiritual possession, an inner apprehension of righteousness with an inner impulse to pursue it. It was conformity in conduct to the law of God, but essentially it was the appropriation of the law by the individual, its integration into his spiritual constitution. The law of God was conceived not as an edict but as an inspiration. In the Prophets' thought, morality is not an offspring of religion but an integral part of it. To 'do judgment and justice', to judge 'the cause of the poor and needy', that is to know God (Jeremiah 22: 15-16). Immediate communion with God brings moral experience, moral knowledge and a moral urge.

Secondly, morality depends on faith in God. Faith in God gives the right sense of values. It dictates the standards and aims for right living. Moreover, to trust God means to have confidence in righteousness. So, the knowledge of God includes a moral dynamism. It generates the power for righteousness. As the Prophets learnt from their personal experience of God, to be aware of Him is to feel the drive to righteousness, because righteousness is in His essence. For the same reason, the converse is true. Right conduct brings men to God. That is why morality belongs to personal religion. The law exalts the spirit of man. The moral qualities it demands in men are those which—in their perfection—are attributed to God; so that when men appropriate it by love and obedience, they take Him into their lives and enter His life. 'I will betroth thee unto me in righteousness, and in judgment, and in loving-kindness and in mercies. I will even betroth thee unto me in faithfulness, and thou shalt know the Lord' (Hosea 2: 19-20). Faith in God and morality are so integrated in the Prophets' thought that faith begets morality and morality has the quality of faith. Morality is thus conduct in a spiritual framework, infused with a spiritual essence, possessing a spiritual power. And because of this valuation of morality, the Prophets exhorted to a higher morality than social convention approved. Righteousness is more than decency. It is obedience to the law of God, not mere conformity with the approved ways of men. The Prophets in their time had to contend against a morality which was not good enough to establish, or express, men's relation to God. Religion at all times has to fight that battle. The Prophets were first to recognise the need to fight it. Their experience of God taught them. The God of righteousness demands more from men than men demand from one another. The good life as conceived by religion requires conduct that accords with the righteousness of God.

Right conduct comprises social and personal morality. It consists of just and loving acts towards others, and also of private behaviour. The Prophets denounced the rich for their rapacity, and also for their luxurious and irresponsible living. 'Woe unto them that rise up early in the morning, that they may follow strong drink; that tarry late into the night, till wine inflame them' (Isaiah 5: 11). 'Woe unto them that are mighty to drink wine and men of strength to mingle strong drink' (Isaiah 5: 22). For such orgies the rich use the wealth they get through oppression. Drunkenness and frivolity are evils in themselves, and they lead to other evils. 'Woe to the crown of pride of the drunkards of Ephraim, and to the fading flower of his glorious beauty, which is on the head of the fat valley of them that are overcome with wine' (Isaiah 28: 1). Significantly, these people have a supercilious and scoffing attitude to religion. 'Whom will he (the Prophet) teach knowledge? and whom will he make to understand his message? them that are weaned from the milk, and drawn from the breasts' (Isaiah 28: 9). Debauchery, unrighteousness and irreligion belong together in the human situation.

Another element in the Prophets' teaching has tended to obscure their stress on personal religion; that is their concern with the life of the nation. Their prophecies, however, about political and social conditions do not, in the framework of their thought, imply the slightest derogation from the importance which should be given to the religious quality in the lives of individuals. On the contrary, their philosophy of the relation between the community and the individual enhanced the importance of personal religion by giving it a collective, as well as an individual, relevance; it affected the destiny of the nation.

Zephaniah sums up the requirements of the good life in two (Hebrew) words. 'Seek righteousness, seek meekness' (Zephaniah 2: 3). Meekness is the humility of piety, which is centred in faith. Personal religion is the supreme value in human life. Without it men lack the full essence of their humanity; they are spiritually immature. Unless men know God, say the Prophets, their lives must wither, being without roots. But when they know God, they have in them the source of life. 'Blessed is the man that trusteth in the Lord, and whose hope the Lord is. For he shall be as a tree planted by the waters and that spreadeth out his roots by the river, and shall not fear when heat cometh but his leaf shall be green; and shall not be careful in the year of drought; neither shall cease from yielding fruit' (Jeremiah 17: 7f). In the thought of all the Prophets, the right personal attitude to God is the fundamental, the essential, quality in the good life.

Faith must live at its centre to dominate it—a dynamic awareness of His being, which engages and exercises the whole of the personality. Through righteousness, men establish their personal relation with God. By righteousness they come to Him, and when they experience Him they are impelled to righteousness. The good life is the life with God in faith and righteousness. Personal religion comprises both—devotion to God and obedience to the moral law. And devotion to God is the motive for obedience to the moral law. He 'delights' (to use Jeremiah's word) in men's goodness.

SEVEN

A JUST SOCIETY

SOCIAL ideals hold a large place in the teaching of the Prophets. Ethical principles must inform the social order and ethical duties be fulfilled by society. They are summed up in the phrase 'social justice'. It requires the right quality in the corporate life of the community; right, according to the moral law.

The Prophets thought of the community as an organic entity, possessing a moral and spiritual quality. This conception of community has a logical justification. A society is more than the sum of the lives of its individuals, just as a circle is more than the sum of the points in its circumference. When individuals constitute a community something comes into being which not only comprehends but also transcends them. This organic idea of community has also a moral justification. A completely moral life for an individual requires a community; it cannot be lived in isolation. Justice and love can be practised only in a community. They describe relations between individuals. But they also describe a quality in the collective or corporate life of a society. A society can, therefore, be moral or immoral. Such a judgment can be made only of a unitary organism capable of a directed collective life. It can not be said of a machine or an instrument. If society were only an organisation which men have developed so that they can live together without plundering or killing one another, then it could not be judged by moral standards but only by its functional efficiency. But a social order can, and should, be judged by moral and spiritual standards because it is an integral human organism.

The Prophets' conception of society developed the idea of group solidarity which had come down from the early stages in human history. The first societies were families where common descent produced naturally the feeling of integral unity. The individuals of a family were 'members of one another' by birth. The consequent feeling of solidarity was taken over into each larger group as it developed out of, and combined, the preceding small groups; from the family into the clan, from the clan into the tribe, and from the tribe into the nation. As originally conceived this solidarity was a physical fact working mechanically. A transgression by one member of a tribe automatically laid the guilt on the whole tribe. But the Prophets moralised it. Unconsciously, but significantly and effectively, they translated it into a spiritual fact, The physical consequences of solidarity remained; but they were put into a spiritual and moral context. The individual shares in, and by his conduct contributes to, the fortunes and misfortunes of the community. All its members suffer for the wickedness of the wicked, and, it should be added, though the idea does not emerge often, that all share in the consequences of the righteousness of the righteous. The Prophets stressed mostly the effect on the nation of the wickedness of some of its members, because they strove to stimulate religious and moral reform. The collective effect of the righteousness of individuals is implied in the explanation and purpose which the poems of the suffering servant give for the servant's suffering.

The use which those whom Jeremiah and Ezekiel

addressed made of the idea of solidarity revealed its danger. When the Prophets threatened that the spiritual faults and moral vices of the people would bring destruction on the nation, the people anwered them with the proverb: 'The fathers have eaten sour grapes and the children's teeth are set on edge', either to exonerate themselves from blame for the impending calamity or to plead impotence to avert it, since according to the proverb its causes lay in the unalterable past. The proverb gave them both an alibi and an excuse for moral inertia. The Prophets answered them by refuting the proverb. But in denying its moral implications for the immediate situation, they could not have intended to reject the idea, and deny the potency, of historical continuity; they could only have meant that each generation has, by its moral character, sufficient power within the historical process to influence its direction, so that it must accept responsibility for its fate. The general tenor of their teaching clearly implies the doctrine of corporate responsibility (cf. Ezekiel 16, 20: 47, 21: 3ff). Individual responsibility did not negate the fact of solidarity.

The solidarity of the community does not, however, relieve the individual of responsibility for his own fate. The Prophets must have meant that the life of the individual is affected by two causes, by the life of the community and by his own character and conduct. Conversely the life of the community is affected by the lives of individuals, who, therefore, cannot be exonerated from responsibility for its fate. It would have cut the ground from under the Prophets' pleadings and admonitions to reject the idea of solidarity. But they combined it with emphasis on individual responsibility.

Because of their conception of community, the

Prophets ascribed moral and spiritual significance to the corporate life of the nation, so that it represented, in their thought, like human personality, an ultimate value. For them ultimate value lay in the right relation with God. The community was therefore required to maintain the kind of collective life which would put it into the right relation with God. 'The Lord will establish thee for an holy people unto himself . . . . if thou wilt keep his commandments and walk in his ways' (Deuteronomy 28: 9 cf. Exodus 19: 5f) is addressed to the totality of Israel. The writer, or speaker, who ascribed that declaration to God had primarily in mind the people collectively as well as persons individually. Translated into the simple language of religion, the Prophets' doctrine about community means that God is interested in the collective life of human societies, and that society can, and ought, by the righteousness of its collective life, relate itself to Him. A nation must constitute itself a society ordered according to the moral law. It was an element in the Prophets' thought, and has remained a distinctive doctrine of Judaism that human society as well as human personality is the object of divine concern.

The stress which the Prophets put on the life of the community did not imply a devaluation of the individual. The responsibility and the dignity of persons are not swamped by the high valuation given to the organic life of society. The Prophets' framework of thought precluded the dichotomy of society and the individual with an implied antithesis between them. They could not think of the community without at the same time thinking of its members individually, and they could not think of the individual without surrounding him by the community. Besides the direct relation between individuals and God there is also the mediate relation between them through the community. When the sun shines on a group collectively it shines also on the individuals in it individually. So God's love towards a community reaches its members individually. Similarly, when a group collectively turns towards God, every member in it is personally looking towards Him. The individual therefore has a two-fold responsibility to correspond with his two-fold relation to God. He shares in the responsibility for the moral quality in the life of the community and he has an immediate personal responsibility. His personal destiny depends on his character and conduct, but they also affect the destiny of the community. The righteousness of a nation is more than the righteousness of individuals, but it must include individual righteousness. So, too, the unrighteousness of a community is more than the unrighteousness of individuals, but it is in the first place the wickedness of individuals 'writ large'. It sums up the Prophets' view fairly to say that they so identified the individual and the community that individual responsibility blended into the responsibility of the community and the responsibility of the community lay on each individual.

The covenant idea, the doctrine of a special relation between God and Israel, combines the responsibility of the individual and the collective responsibility of the community. The covenant binds Israel collectively but it engages each individual in Israel. Its obligations lay on the community as an organic society and on each individual in his personal life. And the nation corporately and its individuals personally could through it establish their relation with God. Every individual in Israel shared in it through membership in the community which in this way mediated his approach to God. At the same time he could, by fulfilling personally its terms, establish himself individually and immediately in relation with God.

The fundamental and universal idea that emerges from the Prophets' thought is that God is concerned with human societies and persons. The two could be morally unified because both were subject to the moral law. The condition for the relation with God was the same for both—the fulfilment of His law by practising righteousness, the community in its social order, the individual by his personal conduct. And both will be brought under God's judgment. He will judge nations according to the righteousness of their social order, and all individuals for the moral quality of their personal lives. Thus, the emphasis which the Prophets put on the collective life of human societies does not exclude appreciation for the high significance of the individual in relation to God; and their concern for the spiritual and moral life of the individual does not ignore, or push aside, the moral value in the collective life of society. Their attention to society does not reduce the individual to a mere cog in a machine; and their concern for the individual does not reduce society to a mere machine. The law fuses the individual and the community into a moral unity. The dichotomy, individual and society, is dissolved under the dominion of the law of God. It commands respect for the life, dignity and rights of human being; it imposes social duties on individuals. Under the moral law, individual righteousness and social justice work together to give the individual his rights and society its righteousness. Conflicts between the rights of individuals and the needs of society could not arise in the thought of the Prophets because the law of God covered them both. The rights of individuals were guaranteed by the obligations laid on society, and the needs of society were met by the duties commanded to individuals.

I have used interchangeably 'community', 'society' and 'nation' not only because they are related, but, practically, the same concept. The State enters into this concept as the instrument of society, or, in other words, as the political organisation of the nation-community. It is functional while the community is organic. It has the function to establish the nation in relation with God by making it a community with a just social order, a community with a collective life dominated by social justice.

What did the Prophets mean by social justice? Consideration for the human rights of all men with special attention to the rights and needs of society's weaker members. They therefore condemned, often vehemently and passionately, the social conditions which bore heavily on the poor. The author of Deuteronomy states explicitly the idea which underlies the Prophets' social teaching. 'For the Lord your God . . . . doth execute the judgment of the fatherless and widow, and loveth the stranger, in giving him food and raiment. So you should love the stranger' (Deuteronomy 10: 17ff). The fundamental principle of social justice is also laid down in the social legislation in Leviticus: 'That thy brother may live with thee' (Leviticus 25: 36). Justice requires care for the weak. Men's needs constitute a claim on society. The Prophets were animated by a pained sympathy for the poor, who suffered from the rapacity of the rich, the venality of judges, the neglect or despotism of rulers. Such poverty and misery presented a religious challenge. Why in a world ruled by a loving and just God did men and women suffer, without any moral fault in themselves, the miseries and hardships of poverty? And the Prophets answered:

Because the social order was wrong, it did not promote justice, but neglected the rights and needs of its weaker members, and allowed the rich and the strong to oppress them.

Ancient Israel had a simple economic system; it was based on agriculture with a superstructure of commerce and handicrafts. All were constituted mainly of small undertakings conducted by individuals with or without employed labour. The labour was supplied by day-labourers, workers hired for longer terms, like a year, and slaves. The treatment of employees was regulated by law, but depended largely on the moral character or social conscience of the employer, who had power over others which he could exercise considerately or oppressively.

The attendant legal system intensified the weakness of the weak and enhanced the power of the strong. As in other agrarian societies, the gravest evils occurred in connection with land ownership. Most people could have economic independence only if they owned land. Ezekiel's constitution for the restored commonwealth, therefore, gives land-ownership special protection. 'Moreover the prince shall not take of the people's inheritance, to thrust them out of their possession; he shall give inheritance to his sons out of his own possession that my people be not scattered every man from his possession' (Ezekiel 46: 18). In Micah's ideal future, 'they shall sit every man under his vine and under his fig tree; and none shall make them afraid' (Micah 4: 4). The Utopia in Leviticus 25 is based on a law which enjoins the permanent land distribution which—theoretically—was to be made when the Hebrews settled in Palestine, so that all should have permanently the economic basis for living. Land was, however, because of its paramount economic importance, the way to wealth, and, therefore, the chief object of acquisitiveness.

The position of the smallholder was extremely precarious. If through a bad harvest, illness, or any other misfortune, he had to borrow money or food from a richer neighbour, he sometimes had to pay a heavy interest. So Amos denounces those who 'trample upon the poor, and take exactions from him of wheat' (Amos 5: 11). But, even worse, an unscrupulous lender might make the conditions for a loan so onerous that it would ultimately bring him the possession of the borrower's land. 'Woe unto them that join house to house, that lay field to field' (Isaiah 5: 8). 'Woe to them that devise iniquity and work evil upon their beds! when the morning is light, they practise it, because it is in the power of their hand. And they covet fields, and seize them; and houses, and take them away: and they oppress a man and his house, even a man and his heritage' (Micah 2: 1f). The poor tenant farmer, prevented by a bad harvest or other misfortune from paying his rent, might not only lose his farm but be compelled to pay his debt by his and his children's slave labour. 'Then there arose a great cry of the people and of their wives against their brethren the Jews. For there were that said, We, our sons and our daughters, are many: let us get corn, that we may eat and live. Some also there were that said, We are mortgaging our fields, and our vineyards, and our houses: let us get corn, because of the dearth. There were also that said, we have borrowed money for the king's tribute upon our fields and our vineyards. Yet now our flesh is as the flesh of our brethren, our children as their children, and lo, we bring unto bondage our sons and our daughters to be slaves and some of our daughters are brought into bondage already; neither is it in our power to help it; for other men have our fields and our vineyards' (Nehemiah 5: 1ff, cf, Jeremiah 34: 8ff). The troubles of the poor farmers spurred Micah to his mission.

The Prophets' strictures against social evils were not directed only against individuals who perpetrated them but also against the system which allowed them, and, worse still, upheld them by laws and by the legal judgments of courts. It was the normal system agrarian communities; the acts which the Prophets denounced were its normal accompaniment, they were not generally considered wrong. The landlord had the right to charge what rent he could enforce, the moneylender to extract any amount of interest he could impose on a borrower who needed the loan to buy food for his family or seed for his land, and the mortgagor had the right to foreclose the mortgage if not paid when due. But to the Prophets, laws which allowed such powers and even enforced them, and the social system to which they pertained were damnably iniquitous. 'Woe unto them that decree unrighteous decrees, and to the writers that write perverseness; to turn aside the needy from judgment, and to take away the right of the poor of my people, that widows may be their spoil, and that they may make the fatherless their prey' (Isaiah 10: 1f). The social system oppressed the poor, by giving to property rights which violated their human rights.

The inference that the Prophets in their social teaching attacked the social system is borne out by their positive demands for social reforms. Amos urged: 'Hate the evil, and love the good, and establish justice in the gate' (Amos 5: 15). 'Justice in the gate' meant to the Prophets, and to the people they addressed, laws and judgments which expressed consideration for the rights and needs of the weaker members of society.[1] Poverty was a social problem, requiring a religious solution. The simple political and economic organisation of society in the time of the Prophets should have made it comparatively easy to apply in its collective life the moral standards imposed by religion. But the historic fact is that the Prophets interpreted the moral principles which regulated the simple nomadic society of the early Hebrews—Jeremiah called them 'the ancient paths'—for the more complicated social life of an agricultural community. The evils they saw spurred them with a sense of moral urgency. Their religious faith was painfully disturbed by the iniquities in the social order which resulted from the power given to the rich to oppress the poor. They pleaded, therefore, for a just society, which restricts the rights of property in order to protect the rights of persons.

There was another aspect of their social teaching. Justice requires that society should provide for the needs of its weaker members. 'To judge the cause of the needy' meant more than to protect them from oppression by the strong and rich. It meant also to protect them against want, to supply them with the means of livelihood. The social reforms which the Prophets urged were intended to fulfil these two requirements of social justice, protection and support of the weak.

Social justice was not, however, for them an end in itself. They were not primarily social reformers. They demanded social reform as an integral part in religious reform. Their humanitarianism inhered in their apprehension of, and devotion to, God. God demanded social justice. By it a nation would bind itself corporately to Him. Religion, therefore, lays on government the obligation to promote social justice.

[1] See pages 92ff.

EIGHT

RELIGION AND POLITICS

It follows from the Prophets' social teaching that government must be directed by religion. In the name of religion they admonished kings; the theocratic idea gave them authority to do so. But their admonitions and exhortations to rulers imply a conception of government which has permanent relevance and validity. The moral quality in the life of a nation is derived not only from the relations between its individual members, but also, and essentially, from the policies and laws of its government. Good government is not only regulative but reformative. Its first duty is to establish social justice. The Prophets may have been right or wrong in ascribing this function to government, but it follows inevitably from their conception of community applied to the nation. Government expresses by its laws and policies a nation's collective character. The State is the community in action; government is its instrument. It is, like persons, bound by the moral law.

The form of government in the time of the Prophets made it easy for them to subject it to spiritual and moral judgment. Government was personal, vested in an absolute monarch. The king ruled, with or without the advice of princes, as he chose; and judges appointed by him constituted the courts. Laws were made by the decisions of judges or the edicts of kings. The religious standards which applied to the conduct of individuals in their private lives could also be applied to government. Righteous government meant a righteous king. Government, or the State, as we know it, is, however, impersonal. That has led to a conception of it as a mere machine, with the consequent danger that it is removed from the scope of the moral law. Translated from the language of monarchy to that of democracy, the Prophets' idea is that government is the agent of the community, obligated to fulfil the responsiblity which the moral law imposes on society. This is the religious ground for the welfare state. The Prophets called for it.

In the utterances addressed to kings and princes, they enunciated clearly and emphatically the function of government to establish a just society. 'Thus saith the Lord; Execute ye judgment and righteousness, and deliver the spoiled out of the hand of the oppressor; and do no wrong, do no violence, to the stranger, the fatherless, nor the widow, neither shed innocent blood in this place' (Jeremiah 22: 3). Government that neglects to provide for the needs of the needy fails in its duty. 'Son of man, prophesy against the shepherds (rulers) of Israel, prophesy, and say unto them, even to the shepherds, 'Thus saith the Lord God: Woe unto the shepherds of Israel that do feed themselves! should not the shepherds feed the sheep? Ye eat the fat, and ye clothe you with the wool, ye kill the fatlings; but ye feed not the sheep. The diseased have ye not strengthened, neither have ye healed that which was sick, neither have ye bound up that which was broken, neither have ye brought again that which was driven away, neither have ye sought that which was lost; but with force and with rigour have ye ruled over them' (Ezekiel 34: 2-4). The specific charge that the rulers lived luxuriously while their subjects suffered deprivations and hardship had absolute monarchy for its context; but the Prophet enunciates a principle valid for all forms of government. Government is not merely an expedient to regulate the life of the community, but the instrument to express its spiritual and moral quality. Its function is not merely to give individuals the freedom and the security to which they are entitled, keeping in restraint aggressive tendencies and competitive selfishness, but also to create a community life with the quality necessary for its relation with God.

The failure of democratic governments to fulfil adequately their social function has brought democracy into jeopardy. It has weakened the moral authority of government and produced, or helped to produce, a reaction in which government in the name of community tramples on the rights and lives of men. In accordance with the Prophets' thought, which makes both persons and communities subject to God's law, the authority of the community was limited by respect for the rights of men, and the rights of men limited by responsibility for the community's righteousness. This general principle gives a practical solution for the problem of individual freedom. The freedom of the individual under the moral law ends where the duty of the community under the moral law begins, and the authority of the community stops where the fundamental rights of the individual come in.

The connection between religion and politics has been disturbed, or obscured, in the democratic countries by two factors which the Prophets did not have to consider; the danger that a religious organisation might use politics to further its own interests or power, and the fact that politics has come to mean a mere conflict between parties for the reins of government. Politics to the Prophets was concerned wholly with questions of right and wrong in the policies of government, so that it came directly under the judgment of religion. True, for them religion was the revelation they received through inspiration. Though individuals cannot now claim such authority, religion must exercise the right, and fulfil the duty, to judge the policies of government by its standards; and its interpreters are entitled to speak in its name, with the condition that they are guided by it, and by nothing else.

In the ideal future, government will fulfil its social function. 'Behold, a king shall reign in righteousness, and princes shall rule in justice' (Isaiah 32: 1). The ideal ruler will guard the rights of society's weaker members, 'With righteousness shall he judge the poor, and reprove with equity for the meek of the earth' (Isaiah 11: 4). A poet, probably celebrating the birth of an heir to the throne, praises him by predicting that his rule will be characterised by justice. 'Of the increase of his government and of peace there shall be no end, upon the throne of David,[1] and upon his kingdom, to establish it, and to uphold it with justice and with righteousness from henceforth even for ever'. (Isaiah 9: 7).

To establish the nation, as a corporate entity, in the right relation with God requires not only justice in its social order but also the direction of its whole life by faith in God. Religion must dominate all politics. God was the ruler of the nation, with prophets as His agents. Rule by prophets, as by Samuel, preceded rule by kings.

In theory the Hebrews remained a theocracy, even after the establishment of the monarchy, in two ways. The king ruled by divine authority, and he was

[1] All the sovereigns of Judaea, the southern kingdom of Hebrews, belonged to the dynasty of David.

subject to divine authority exercised through prophets. The theocratic idea endowed the prophet with a political function. With devout kings he held the key position. Neither politics, nor any other aspect of human life, fell outside the prophets' sphere; nothing could be outside the concern or the dominion of God. So, Zechariah led a political movement to restore the monarchy by making Zerubbabel king after the return of the exiles from Babylonia. And all the prophets 'engaged in politics'.

The concern of the Prophets with questions which might be described as purely political, and the grounds for it, appear most clearly in their judgments on alliances with other countries. Hosea condemned the government of the northern kingdom under Jeroboam II for its shifting alliances with Egypt and Assyria. 'And Ephraim is like a silly dove, without understanding; they call unto Egypt, they go to Assyria' (Hosea 7: 11). Isaiah's first sermon, to King Ahaz, dealt with a political crisis (chapter 7) and throughout his ministry he opposed any suggested alliance whether with Assyria or Egypt. So, too, Jeremiah opposed alliances with these countries. 'And now what hast thou to do in the way to Egypt . . . . . . or what hast thou to do in the way to Assyria . . .?' (Jeremiah 2: 18). 'Why gaddest thou about so much to change thy way? thou shalt be ashamed of Egypt also, as thou wast of Assyria' (Jeremiah 2: 36); and later, he opposed the suggestion to call in the aid of Egypt, or to make an alliance with surrounding nations, against Babylonia (chapter 27). Similarly, Ezekiel condemned those who sought help from Egypt in a plan to rebel against Babylonia. 'But he (Zedekiah, King of Judah) rebelled against him (the king of Babylonia) in sending his ambassadors into Egypt, that they might give him horses and much people. Shall he prosper? shall he escape that doeth such things? shall he break the covenant, and yet escape?' (Ezekiel 17: 15).

Conceivably, the Prophets' appraisal of the international situation may underlie their view that entanglements with other nations could only bring disaster to Palestine. Being the cockpit of the world, it might, in the long run, have the best promise of security in neutrality. It may also be that the Prophets' opposition to alliances was actuated by the fear, conscious or unconscious, that they would contaminate the religion of the Hebrews with influences from the idolatries of the allied peoples. But they clearly had deeper reasons. Alliances showed disloyalty towards God, or rebellion against His rule. They relied on physical power. They are like idolatry; both exalt the physical. Both turn away from God. An alliance with a military power showed a lack of faith in Him. 'Thus saith the Lord: Cursed is the man that trusteth in man. and maketh flesh his arm, and whose heart departeth from the Lord' (Jeremiah 17: 5). 'For my people have committed two evils; they have forsaken me the fountain of living waters, and hewed them out cisterns, broken cisterns, that can hold no water' (Jeremiah 2: 13). Like idolatry, alliances are described as a wife's unfaithfulness to her husband. 'Thou hast also committed fornication with the Egyptians, thy neighbours, great of flesh; and hast multiplied thy whoredom, to provoke me to anger' (Ezekiel 16: 26, cf. Chapter 23). And like idolatry, alliances sabotaged true religion. For the people to think that alliances could save them would withdraw attention from the importance of righteousness in their personal lives and in the government of the nation. 'Woe to them that go down to Egypt for help, and stay on horses; and trust in chariots, because they are many, and in horsemen, because they are very strong; but they look not unto the Holy One of Israel, neither seek the Lord' (Isaiah 31: 1). So when Israel turns to God in repentance, it will no longer trust to alliances and military power, nor worship idols. 'Assyria shall not save us; we will not ride upon horses, neither will we say any more to the works of our hand, Ye are our gods, for in thee the fatherless findeth mercy' (Hosea 14: 3).

Of course, the Prophets thought alliances futile. Since they were contrary to the will of God, the political wisdom which valued them was stupid. Military power cannot give a guarantee of security. If the nation relies on the violent methods of power, it will come to disaster. For Judah to ally itself with Syria and Israel against Assyria, instead of following a policy of peace, will only bring a devastating invasion by Assyria. 'For as much as this people hath refused the waters of Shiloah that go softly, and rejoice in Rezin (the King of Syria), and Remaliah's son (the King of Israel), now therefore, behold, the Lord bringeth up upon them the waters of the river, strong and many, even the King of Assyria and all his glory: and he shall come up over all his channels, and go over all his banks' (Isaiah 8: 6-7). Strength comes from faith in God; so a nation can attain security only by policies directed by such a faith (Isaiah 7: 9).

Because of that faith Isaiah maintained that Jerusalem, being the centre of the worship of the true God, could not be destroyed. That belief received signal justification in 701 B.C. when, for no reason that could be seen by the people of Jerusalem, Sennacherib's army, which besieged the city, retired suddenly and secretly in the night. The incident, historically verified, raises some interesting questions, but it would be precarious to base on it any suggestion about prophecy generally or Isaiah's prognosticating power in particular. The event occurred, but the story that Isaiah predicted it may be a later legend; but even if the story is historical, it would prove no more than Isaiah's strong faith. The definite predictions of the Prophets were not always fulfilled, and Isaiah's belief that Jerusalem could not be destroyed was disproved a little more than a century later. But in this belief Isaiah expressed his faith in God. Though sinful, Jerusalem was needed to serve God's purpose, that all humanity should ultimately worship Him. Isaiah may have been right. Had Judaea been destroyed in his time, it might well have suffered the same fate as the northern Hebrew kingdom which was destroyed then and disappeared from history for ever, leaving behind only its name; the ten lost tribes. The religion of the Jews was still bound up with a national framework; it had not yet attained to the full consciousness and strength of its distinctiveness.

Jeremiah, on the other hand, could dispense with Jerusalem. The religious situation had changed: Judaism did not need an inviolable physical centre. The Prophets who preceded him had made it a unique religion. Their teaching took firm root; even though they complained that it was unheeded. Judaism, the religion of monotheism, was a firmer, stronger reality in Jeremiah's time than in Isaiah's, because of the work of Isaiah and his contemporary prophets, Hosea, Amos and Micah. Though their time was followed by an orgy of idolatry in the reign of Manasseh, induced by his desire to curry favour with the conquering Assyrians, their teaching was not lost, as Josiah's reformation showed. Jeremiah, therefore, could deny Isaiah's doctrine that Jerusalem and its Temple could not be destroyed; on the contrary, he threatened that they would be.

For the same reason, that Judaism was firmly established, he minimised the significance of the Babylonian invasion and conquest of Judaea. He advised surrender because resistance was useless—it would only waste human lives—the Babylonians would certainly conquer the city, since God was using them. It was futile for the unrighteous to try to avert the consequences of their unrighteousness by military efforts; they could save themselves only by repentance. He had also another reason. Nothing of fundamental importance could be gained by resistance. To yield to Babylonia meant paying tribute. That did not matter. The religion was not at stake, and if they were taken into exile, they could still maintain their religion in another land (Jeremiah 29). What was most valuable in the life of the Jews, their religion, could not be hurt by political subjugation to the rule of Babylonia (Jeremiah 27). Judaism had burst out of its national tegument. Monotheism had inevitably developed its universal scope.

But did not Jeremiah's advice not to resist the Babylonians show a lack of patriotism? The answer involves a valuation of nationalism. Nationalism, in the modern sense, that is, as a political fact, was unknown to the ancient Hebrews, or to any people in the ancient world. The 'nation' comprised a religion, political unity and often common descent. For the most part, it meant only a group inhabiting a land under one ruler, and having a common religion. For the Prophets religion had the central place in the Hebrew nation. All their thought about Israel has to be understood in the light of their belief that it was a people of religion. Hence its election. Hence, too, religion was its life as a people. It had to live by faith. 'This is the word of the Lord unto Zerubbabel, saying, Not by might, nor by power, but by my spirit saith the Lord of hosts' (Zechariah 4: 6).

In so far as the Prophets gave any value to the political existence of the Hebrew people, it was derived from the religious significance they attached to it. A few passages in the books of the Prophets suggest a kind of national chauvinism, probably in reaction to national misfortune, or to oppression by a foreign ruler; but even they have an underlying religious motive, though expressed unfortunately. The 'new Jerusalem' symbolises, in its physical greatness and beauty, a high spiritual exaltation. Generally, Israel is, in the thought of the Prophets, a people of religion, that is, a group based on a distinctive religion, with a religious purpose and a corresponding religious function, in its separate existence.

Though in the framework of the Prophets' thought, ultimate religious attainment would bring also material blessing, it was the religious life of the nation that concerned them. They opposed policies motivated by a merely political nationalism. 'Ephraim he mixeth himself among the peoples. Ephraim is a cake not turned . . . And the pride of Israel doth testify to his face, yet they have not returned unto the Lord their God, nor sought him, for all this' (Hosea 7: 8f). Because they trust to their half-baked international politics, mixing among the nations as if they were an important nation, they do not seek God; their political nationalism had supplanted religion. That is, unfortunately, a common phenomenon, and the Prophets would have condemned it wherever it occurred. But it troubled them especially in Israel's case because of the universal religious purpose they ascribed to Israel's existence. The patriotism of the Prophets was a love of their people expressed in the passionate desire to exalt its life in faith and righteousness.

Jeremiah's attitude might be interpreted as basically pacifist, but it emerged from his reading of history and his conception of Israel's place in it. Isaiah's pronouncements, especially when Sennacherib was besieging Jerusalem, might also be interpreted as pacifism. But it may be doubted whether the interpretation, though tenable and even plausible, would be correct. True, he proclaims explicitly the basic idea of pacifism: 'Trust in God and do not fight'; but he was motivated not by a religious objection to war—for he says that the warring Babylonians are an instrument in God's hand—but by his confident faith.

Faith in God is the paramount teaching of the Prophets. All their other teachings flow from it. And they applied it to politics. By the standards it imposes, they laid on government the duty to create a just society. It dictated their opposition to alliances. The permanent truth in that opposition is the judgment on power politics. They condemned it not only because it was futile, but also, and even more, because it was, from the theistic point of view, morally wrong. It showed a trust in physical strength, putting it above the faith which exalts spiritual values, and it defied, or violated, the rule of God. Politics in all its phases must be guided by religion; it must pursue righteousness under the influence of faith in God. Otherwise it will bring a nation to disaster. The Prophets attained to this truth through inspired thought and proved its validity by their reading of history, the history of their own people and of all nations.

NINE

TRUE RELIGION

THE Prophets had attained a new conception of religion, which they strove, eagerly and passionately, to impress on their contemporaries. The progress of human thought,—it may fairly be said under the Prophets' influence—has turned their idea of true religion into a truism, in their time it was new and revolutionary. In general terms it can be defined very simply. True religion is the knowledge of the true God and obedience to His law. The simplicity of the definition conceals, however, much complexity in each of its two elements.

The knowledge of the true God meant, in the first place, a realisation and awareness of the One God who is the Creator and Ruler of the universe. That is monotheism. It is a vitally important belief, because true religion must begin with the right conception of God. From it issues the right understanding of the universe and of man's place in it. Secondly, the knowledge of God includes an apprehension of His moral attributes. As the Prophets themselves were impressed profoundly and mightily by His righteousness, they wanted all men to be similarly impressed, so that they would, under His impulsion and guidance, pursue righteousness. Thirdly, the knowledge of God culminates in an intimate personal relation with Him, established by and infused with loving devotion towards Him.

True religion consists of faith and morality, not merely related, with the second dependent on the first but woven together into a unity. To know God means to practise righteousness; to practise righteousness inheres in the knowledge of God. Logic may separate them for analysis; in true religion they are one and inseparable. They are so intertwined that morality belongs to the spiritual constitution of man. That is what Jeremiah meant by the law written in the heart. His prophecy of the new covenant affirms the universal truth that the sense of personal relation with God produces spontaneously the religious, and therefore the moral, way of life. Faith includes both moral direction and moral compulsion. Conversely, morality at its best has the inwardness of faith.

Because faith in God and morality are inextricably interwoven, morality has no basis outside religion. Ways of conduct may be approved if they follow an established social pattern; but ways of righteousness need deeper, much deeper, direction. A social pattern may not be morally good enough, it may lack righteousness or love. The moral evils which the Prophets condemned comprised conduct which followed the existing social pattern. They demanded a higher morality. This higher morality must derive its instruction and impulsion from religion. It depends on a sense of duty. Its verb is 'ought' not 'is done'. The ultimate sanction for an 'ought' is the moral order of the universe. That is why it needs religion to enforce it.

On the whole, experience has proved the validity of the prophetic doctrine that morality can exist only in religion. Professed adherents of religion who have violated moral principles only prove that their human weakness is stronger than their religion. On the other hand, the conspicuousness of their moral failure proves that strict conformity with high moral principles belongs to religion. Those away from religion who have practised a high morality do not disprove the connection between them; they may be dominated by the influence of an inherited religious legacy.

The unbreakable connection between religion and morality is affirmed in the Prophets' paramount doctrine about the law of God. It teaches man to know the true God, to have faith in Him, and to do what is right and avoid what is wrong in His sight. Faith and right conduct are integrally united. The right attitude to God and righteousness in living—that is the law of God; to possess it inwardly and to follow it outwardly—that is true religion.

The integral and high place which the Prophets give to morality in true religion has been misinterpreted to suggest that they defined religion as ethics and made ethics the whole content of religion. They excluded special acts of worship, like sacrifices, from true religion, or gave them only a subsidiary place, to emphasise the supreme importance of righteousness; but righteousness belonged to the relation with God. The burning passion with which they proclaim its demands on persons and society is generated by the conviction that morality is the way for men individually and society collectively to put themselves right with God, to establish their relation with Him.

True religion must contend, however, against false religion. Gresham's law operates also in religion, the false drives out the true. The Prophets' denunciations of the false religion which prevailed in their times derive permanent importance from the fact that they point to dangers which have confronted, and confront, religion at all times.

The books of the Prophets inveigh unwearyingly

against idolatry; it was, in their thought, the chief enemy of true religion. They condemn two kinds of idolatry; one, the worship of idols; the other, the use of idols in the worship of the true God. The worship of idols is an evil in itself, it belongs to polytheism. The Prophets do not distinguish between idolatry and polytheism; they went together. Polytheism is the worship of gods that are not gods, gods that are vanity, non-existent, empty of reality. The idols it used proved its stupidity.

The Hebrews were not free from polytheism and its idolatry. The religions of other peoples influenced them. In Palestine itself, the Canaanitish religion did not end with the settlement of the Hebrews. When the Hebrews infiltrated into Canaan they tended to adopt the Canaanitish worship of Baalim (lords). The conquest of Palestine by the Assyrians produced, in the reign of Manasseh, a veritable orgy of idol worship to conform with the religion of the conqueror. Many of the Jews who were exiled in Babylonia undoubtedly succumbed under the pressure of the environment to the influence of its polytheism. 'That which cometh into your mind shall not be at all; in that ye say, We will be as the nations, as the families of the countries, to serve wood and stone' (Ezekiel 20: 32). When Deutero-Isaiah satirised the gods whom the Babylonians worshipped, he may well have had in mind Jews in Babylonia who followed its religion. When Jeremiah upbraided the Hebrew refugees in Egypt for allowing their wives to offer sacrifices to idols, they answered: 'As for the word that thou hast spoken unto us in the name of the Lord, we will not hearken unto thee. But we will certainly perform every word that is gone forth out of our mouth, to burn incense unto the queen of heaven and to pour out drink offerings unto her, as we have done, we, and our fathers, our kings and our princes, in the cities of Judah, and in the streets of Jerusalem; for then had we plenty of victuals, and were well, and saw no evil. But since we left off to burn incense to the queen of heaven, and to pour out drink offerings unto her, we have wanted all things, and have been consumed by the sword and by the famine' (Jeremiah 44: 16-18).

Even leaders of the community secretly practised idolatry. 'Then said he unto me, Son of man, hast thou seen what the elders of the house of Israel do in the dark, every man in his chambers of imagery? for they say, the Lord seeth us not, The Lord hath forsaken the earth' (Ezekiel 8: 12). Monotheism had not been firmly established among all the Hebrews; many worshipped 'strange gods'. As the defiant refugees in Egypt suggested, they had tradition on their side. The revolutionary doctrine of the Prophets which assailed it had only the authority of their inspiration. From their monotheistic point of view, polytheism was itself false religion; and its falsehood was exposed in its idolatry. The Prophets' objection to idolatrous polytheism was intensified by the immoral and even horrible (Jeremiah 32: 35) practices sometimes associated with it, but the objection itself originated in their passionate monotheism. It put them into uncompromising opposition to the prevalent polytheism of their time which identified idols with gods.

The use of idols had also survived in the Hebrew religion, or crept into it. The bulls which Jeroboam set up in Dan and Bethel were idols in the worship of Jahveh, the God of the Hebrews. A bronze serpent stood in the Temple in Jerusalem until the time of Hezekiah (II Kings 18: 4). Canaanitish religious practices were taken over by the Hebrews when they settled in Canaan. The settlement changed them from nomads into farmers. Quite naturally they felt the need to adapt their religion to the new circumstances; the way was there in the rites of the Canaanitish religion, such as the festivals celebrating the agricultural seasons and rites to invoke fertility. Some of them could be integrated in the Hebrew religion, but others marred it. So religious practices which the Hebrews adopted from the Canaanites had muddled their primitive religion with the impurities of Baal worship. 'According to their pasture, so were they filled; they were filled, and their heart was exalted; therefore have they forgotten me' (Hosea 13: 6). Jeremiah 2: 13 may refer to Baal worship. They forsook God 'the fountain of living waters', and turned to the Baalim who had no life-giving power, being themselves life-less. Though the Canaanites themselves were in the course of time absorbed by the Hebrews, some of their religious beliefs and practices survived, presenting an ever present menace to the distinctive character of Judaism as the Prophets conceived it. As late as the 5th century B.C., the author of the third section in the Book of Isaiah finds it necessary to condemn idolatrous practices.

In the time of the Prophets, the Canaanitish elements in the popular religion of the Hebrews had behind it a tradition of five or more centuries. Hence Jeremiah's rhetorical question: Did the religion of the Hebrews require these things originally? The Prophets were religious revolutionaries, but like other religious reformers they identified progress forward with changes backwards. They opposed the dominant tradition to restore an older, and simpler religion. 'Thus saith the Lord, Stand ye in the ways and see, and ask for the old paths, where is the good way, and walk therein, and ye shall find rest for your souls; but they said, We will not walk therein' (Jeremiah 6: 16). Jeremiah idealised the early religion of the Hebrews; but in this idealisation he saw the true religious tradition.

The Prophets could not allow idols in the worship of the true God. They insisted on His uniqueness and universal sovereignty. He was not just a Baal like the gods which the Canaanites worshipped. He was Lord of the land, but much more, he was Lord of the universe. He could not be worshipped as the Baalim were worshipped by the Canaanites.

So far as the Prophets give us an insight into their underlying thought, they had several grounds for their vehement objection to the use of idols in religion. In the first place, it made Judaism like the other religions, obscuring its protest against polytheism, and endangering its distinctive character. The religion of Baal had idols, the religion of the true God, must, therefore, avoid them. But by the help of later Judaism and some of the Prophets' utterances about God, we can get a glimpse of another reason for their objection to idols in the worship of God, which has permanent relevance to religion. An idol would give physical form to Him who transcends all forms, thereby derogating from His divinity. It made God less than God to represent Him physically. Even to think of Him in human terms violated His character. Idolatry in the worship of the true God misrepresented Him, and it is important spiritually and morally to have the right conception of God. The quality of a religion and its directions for conduct issue from the kind of God it worships.

Two further reasons suggest themselves, with some basis in the Prophets' books, for their objection to idolatry. An idol tends, because of its concreteness, to divert to itself the worship which should be directed to God. In this way it becomes His rival. Hosea, Jeremiah and Ezekiel apply to the worship of idols the epithets that fit an unfaithful wife, or a harlot. They may have referred to the worship of 'strange gods', but it is equally probable that they had in mind the use of idols in the Hebrew religion of their time. The worship of any idol involved disloyalty to the true God.

Moreover, it blocks the way to God in also a deeper sense. It puts a high value on a physical form; thereby weakening the attention to spiritual values which true religion requires. Even, therefore, an idol used in the worship of the true God endangers true religion; it externalises religion, which should be essentially a possession and force in the human spirit.

All these reasons for the Prophets' objection to idols amount to the one reason that practically and psychologically the use of idols prevented the knowledge of God, and obscured the obligation to worship Him by right conduct. It was false religion usurping the place of true religion. Idols either expressed a belief in false gods, and thereby shut out the true God, or by misrepresenting Him, they prevented the faith and hindered the righteousness by which men can bind their lives to Him. True religion requires faith and righteousness; idolatry consisted of magical rites, it was both materialistic and amoral; and its evil was aggravated by, or manifested in, the immorality which sometimes accompanied it.

The reasons which animated the Prophets' attitude to idols had a special cogency in their time; and, it must be recognised, they have some permanent force. They wanted to insist on spiritual reality and moral obligation in their conception of God, and idolatry carried the danger that the spiritual would be obscured by the physical and moral obligation supplanted by ritualism. There have been some adherents of religion who have overcome that danger. It may be that the author of Malachi ignored it; otherwise he could not have written, at a time when all religions except Judaism used idols, that 'From the rising of the sun even unto the going down of the same my name is great among the nations; and in every place incense is offered unto my name, and a pure offering; for my name is great among the nations, saith the Lord of Hosts' (Malachi 1: 11). The crucial test for any form of worship is whether it promotes an apprehension of the ultimacy of spirit and of the paramountcy of spiritual and moral values.

Some of the considerations against idolatry moved some of the Prophets to condemn also ritualism. The chief rites in the times of the Prophets were connected with the Temple, the daily sacrifices, the additional sacrifices on Sabbaths and holy days, and the private sacrifices of individuals. The last were either offerings to atone for sins, or free-will offerings to enable the worshipper to eat meat. Until the time of Deuteronomy, the seventh century B.C., only by making such offerings could meat be obtained which was ritually fit. Hosea, Micah, Jeremiah, Amos and probably Isaiah would have none of these sacrifices. Hosea's famous utterance expresses absolute opposition. God wants loving devotion, not animal sacrifices, and a sense of personal relation to Him rather than those sacrifices which were considered the highest offerings. Sacrifices do not, and cannot, establish the relation with God; 'They shall go with their flocks and with their herds to seek the Lord; but they shall not find him; he hath withdrawn himself from them' (Hosea 5: 6).

The ritual sacrifices cannot serve any good purpose, they cause spiritual harm. 'Because Ephraim hath multiplied altars to sin, altars have been unto him to sin' (Hosea 8: 11). Amos rejects the whole Temple ritual and religious cult. 'I hate, I despise your feasts, and I will take no delight in your solemn assemblies. Yea, though ye offer me your burnt offerings and meal offerings, I will not accept them; neither will I regard the peace offerings of your fat beasts. Take thou away from me the noise of thy songs; for I will not hear the melody of thy viols' (Amos 5: 21-23). Isaiah does not make it clear whether he objects to sacrifices and ceremonies altogether, or only when they are not accompanied by righteous living. There is no ambiguity about Jeremiah's attitude. 'Thus saith the Lord of hosts, the God of Israel: Add your burnt offerings unto your sacrifices, and eat ye flesh. For I spake not unto your fathers, nor commanded them in the day that I brought them out of the land of Egypt, concerning burnt offerings or sacrifices' (Jeremiah 7: 21f.). Nor does Micah leave any doubt about his attitude. 'Wherewith shall I come before the Lord, and bow myself before the high God? shall I come before him with burnt offerings, with calves of a year old? Will the Lord be pleased with thousands of rams or with ten thousands of rivers of oil? shall I give my firstborn for my transgressions, the fruit of my body for the sin of my soul' (Micah 6: 6-7). And the answer is No! God does not want these things. He wants lives of goodness and faith.

Ezekiel, on the other hand, devotes a large part of his book to a plan for a restored Temple in Jerusalem with a system of sacrifices. Haggai urged the returned exiles to rebuild the Temple, blaming their neglect to do so for their hardships and misfortunes. Malachi, too, shows zealous concern for the Temple ritual. On the other hand, the author of the third part of the book of Isaiah, who lived and preached when the Temple had been rebuilt, seems to have had the same attitude to ritualism generally as the earlier Prophets. The right kind of fast, that is, the right way to worship God is to relieve the oppressed and help the needy (Isaiah 58: 5ff). Zechariah expressed a similar view (Zechariah 7: 4ff).

The importance which the author of the third part of the Book of Isaiah and Jeremiah attach to the Sabbath must be explained by its social, rather than its ritual significance; its observance belonged to social morality. It gave slaves and serfs the right to a day of rest. That interpretation is supported by the concern for the rights of slaves which Jeremiah showed in another context (Jeremiah 34: 8ff), and by the general theme of Isaiah 58, which is the social requirements of religion. The Deuteronomic version of the Decalogue states explicitly the social purpose of the Sabbath: 'that thy man slave and maid slave may rest as well as thou'. Isaiah's scorn for the Sabbath and the new moon (Isaiah 1: 13f) was probably directed against the rituals associated with them; he put them with 'the calling of assemblies'.

The divergence in the Prophets' attitude to sacrifices may be due to varying circumstances. On the whole it would appear that when the Temple stood, Prophets either condemned or deprecated its ritual (Malachi may be an exception); but when the Temple was destroyed, Prophets valued it more highly. It may, however, be doubted whether any of them gave ceremonies more than a secondary place in religion. Even Ezekiel who outlines a plan for a restored Temple and its ritual, devotes the larger part of his book to the spiritual and moral demands of religion. Malachi condemns the priests for bringing faulty sacrifices, but he defines the function of the priest in spiritual and moral terms (Malachi 2: 5f). Most of the other Prophets agreed with Hosea's declaration that God desires loyalty in thought, feeling and conduct, not sacrifices, and faith with righteousness rather than burnt offerings; and with Micah's categorical assertion that God does not want ceremonial observances, however elaborate, or perhaps the more elaborate the less He wants them. So the author of the third part of Isaiah makes a contrast between those who want a Temple for sacrifices and the truly pious (Isaiah 66: 5).

The Prophets who condemn sacrifices, whether absolutely or when they are offered by people who ignore the moral demands of religion, imply the objection to religious ceremonies that they tend to detract attention from the more important, the essential, elements in religion, faith and right conduct. In the first place, they do not make a constant demand, they are comparatively easy to perform, and,—perhaps this is the chief ground for the objection,—they can give emotional satisfaction in return for a comparatively small effort, so that they tend to push faith and righteousness out of the paramount place in religion. That is their intrinsic danger; some people 'enjoy' them for themselves. They 'offer a sacrifice of thanksgiving of that which is leavened, and proclaim freewill offerings and publish them, for this liketh you, O ye children of Israel, saith the Lord God' (Amos 4: 5). Hosea 8: 13, it is suggested, should be emended to say: 'They love sacrifices'. Because of the enjoyment derived from religious ceremonials they tend to block the spiritual striving for 'the knowledge of God', and to push aside the moral obligations imposed by 'the law of God'. So Amos, after saying that God hates, and does not want, feasts, sacrifices, and the music that accompanied them, continues: 'But let justice roll down like waters and righteousness like a mighty stream' (Amos 5: 24).

Two further, and related dangers attend the use of ceremonies in religion. They open the descent to formalism which is the enemy of religion, all the more harmful spiritually because it apes religion. It insults God and puts a blight on the spirit of men. The Prophets saw only spiritual degeneration in the formalism 'which swears by the name of the Lord (affirms loyalty to him) but not in truth nor in righteousness' (Isaiah 48: 1). 'And the Lord said, Forasmuch as this people draw nigh unto me, and with their mouth and with their lips do honour me, but have removed their heart from me, and their fear of me is a commandment of men which hath been taught them (that is, learnt by rote) . . . the wisdom of their wise men shall perish' (Isaiah 29: 13f). The Prophets included formal religion among the evils that would destroy the nation. Moreover, ceremonies may engender the belief that they have an intrinsic power, without reference to the spiritual attitude of the worshipper. The Prophets saw the danger actualised. Ritualism materialised religion, making it a kind of magic. In the ideal religion of the future, therefore, even the ark will be a thing of the past, and forgotten (Jeremiah 3: 16). The belief that sacrifices can establish the right relation with God is false in itself and pernicious in its effects.

The fear of the Prophets that religious ceremonials tend to produce a false conception of religion with disastrous spiritual and moral consequences has been justified by facts. On the other hand, religious observances in the name of God (to use a Rabbinic phrase, that is, to express devotion to Him) have frequently conveyed a real stimulus to the religious life. The Prophets, therefore, who valued them may have been moved not by religious conservatism, which merely follows tradition, but by the belief that rites can stimulate the religious consciousness.

Perhaps the Prophets' views about ceremonies may be summed up in a way which will take account of their divergences and bring out their agreement. Men establish their relation with God by faith in Him and righteousness in conduct. They must not delude themselves into thinking that ceremonial observances can establish that relation; even though they may find in such observances a satisfaction which, rightly or wrongly, they take to be spiritual fulfilment. Beyond this point, prophetic thought divides into two views: one that the danger in ceremonial observances outweighs their value; and the other that they should be maintained for their value, presumably with watchfulness to avoid their spiritual and moral harm. The divergence may have been due to a difference in personal temperaments; but it may also represent reactions to different situations. The objection to sacrifices was expressed most vehemently by the Prophets who lived when there was a Temple in Jerusalem, and its ritual was observed. At other times Prophets valued the Temple and its ritual more highly. The divergence accords with a generalisation drawn from experience. When people are 'religious' without being moral, there is need to denounce that kind of religion, but when they are neither religious nor moral, there is the hope that if they can be got to observe special acts of religion, they may so open themselves to its influence that they will follow its instruction to pursue the good life. The outstanding fact in the Prophets' attitude to the ritual side of religion is that their stress on the inwardness of religion made some of them suspicious of all material aids in the approach to God, and their insistence on righteousness made them condemn the ceremonialism which usurped its place.

The true worship of God must engage the whole of life; ritual acts are valuable in so far as they help it, but dangerous because they may stifle it if multiplied excessively or given exaggerated importance. This, I think, is a fair deduction from the Prophets' utterances about sacrifies, fasts and feasts; it is a doctrine which has permanent validity. The worship of God which true religion requires is to love Him and to practise righteousness.

Looked at through the perspective of history the Prophets really tried to produce a development of Judaism to correspond with their monotheism. In their mission to promote true religion, they were faced with the task which often confronts religion, and is as often shirked, the task to develop its thought and worship. Traditional rites can preserve themselves (but not their value) through all changes; but faith must take account of changes in thought. Monotheism involved a fundamental change of thought. The Prophets' conception of God could not tolerate idols nor permit an intrinsic, or magical, value to rituals. He was not that kind of a God.

The Prophets' conception of true religion also included another development, new emphasis on righeousness and new ideas about its practical requirements. In its earlier period the religion of the Hebrews had put much emphasis on justice. Monotheism added force to that emphasis. And social conditions showed the need for a new and enlarged definition of justice, to meet the change from the pastoral to the agricultural way of life. Though the change occurred some centuries before the Prophets, religion had not yet effectively adapted its fundamental moral instruction to the new conditions. The moral injunctions of the older religion were inadequate. Moreover, such adaptations take a long time. Though the industrial revolution began in the early part of the eighteenth century, it may be doubted whether religion has yet developed its social and moral teaching to a form which applies effectively to the ramified economic and financial organisation of an industrial society. The Prophets taught the way to apply the religious principle of justice to the agricultural society of their time.

In their efforts to promote these developments in faith and conduct, the Prophets were opposed by old traditions. In beliefs there were polytheism and idolatry; and in the worship of the true God there was formal ceremonialism. These constituted the false religion against which they had to contend. They also had to contend against the low standards of conventional morality. The law of God requires more than conventional morality. True religion always imposes the duty to examine, and judge, the generally accepted moral standards. Furthermore, they strove to reform a social system which permitted and even fostered social evils. The law of God requires a just society, so true religion must work to create it. The good life for persons and the good society for a nation must be rooted in a dynamic faith in the true God.

TEN

GOD AND HUMAN LIFE

IN their passionate endeavours to establish true religion, the Prophets had to fight on two fronts; they had to combat not only false religion but also irreligion. The irreligion took various forms. The rich, lulled by their prosperity into spiritual apathy, were indifferent to religion, saying that it did not matter, it had no practical significance. They were 'the men that are settled on their lees, they say in their hearts, The Lord will not do good, neither will he do evil' (Zephaniah 1: 12). The unfortunate, disappointed in their hopes, questioned the justice of God. 'Ye have wearied the Lord with your words. Yet ye say, Wherein have we wearied him? In that ye say, every one that doeth evil is good in the sight of the Lord, and he delighteth in them, or where is the God of judgment?' (Malachi 2: 17). And there were those who devoted themselves wholly to the pursuit of pleasure without giving any thought to God. 'And the harp and the lute, the tabret and the pipe, and wine, are in their feasts; but they regard not the work of the Lord, neither have they considered the operation of his hands' (Isaiah 5: 12). 'Let us eat and drink for tomorrow we shall die' (Isaiah 22: 13). They simply mocked at the Prophet who admonished them.

The Prophets did not have to contend against the atheism which denies the existence of God, but against the scepticism which questions, and the hedonism which denies, His government. Both these attitudes evidenced spiritual poverty and produced moral perversity. . . . 'Woe unto them that draw iniquity with cords of vanity (falsehood), and sin as it were with a cart rope: that say, Let him make speed, let him hasten his work, that we may see it: and let the counsel of the Holy One of Israel draw nigh and come, that we may know it!' (Isaiah 5: 18-19). The denial of God's activity in human life cut at the roots of the Prophets' denunciations, pleadings and exhortations. It was a fundamental doctrine of their thought that His moral order dominates the lives of men, nations and humanity. They declared 'God wants you to be righteous'; they were answered: 'God does not care what we are or do. Nothing is to be gained by righteousness. What difference does it make to men whether they do good or evil'? This irreligion supported itself by the frequent discrepancy between men's conduct and their fortunes. The Prophets maintained that righteousness led to happiness and sin to suffering, but facts seemingly refuted their doctrine. The faithful and righteous often suffered, the disbelievers and unrighteous often prospered. Not only does virtue often bring no reward and sin no penalty, but, even worse, the righteous often suffer contumely and oppression from the sinful.

The problem posed for theism by this glaring fact in human life was eased for the Prophets by their conception of community. The connection between morality and prosperity on the one hand, and, on the other, between sin and decay can be traced more easily in the lives of nations than in the lives of individuals. History can be adduced to support the thesis that righteousness exalts a nation and unrighteousness destroys it. The evil consequences of collective sin are obvious. A nation with the rich given to luxury, the poor condemned to misery, and the rulers heedless of their responsibility, or even practising oppression, will collapse through inner corruption or fall an easy prey to attack from without. Just as righteousness strengthens a nation, so unrighteousness rots it. The fate of nations depends on the moral quality of their lives.

The idea of solidarity justified the fact that men shared in the fate of their nation regardless of their own deserts. The individual cannot be treated in isolation. Whatever his own conduct and character, he must feel the consequences of the character and conduct of the community. True, as Jeremiah and Ezekiel insisted, the individual fares as he merits, but at the same time he must also share in the fate which the whole community brings on itself by the character of its collective life. The righteous will survive the collective doom, but they cannot escape suffering. The idea of solidarity could explain, and justify, their suffering when the nation suffered. But it does not completely solve the problem posed by the lack of correspondence between men's virtue and their fortunes. Why do some who are righteous suffer, and some who are wicked prosper normally?

The idea of solidarity did not imply any diminution in God's concern for individuals.[1] The individual has a two-fold relation with God; mediately through the community, and immediately by himself. This two-fold relation brings in two ways the activity of God into the life of the individual. In the first place, the individual shares in God's care for, and interest in, the community. God's love for Israel was both collective and distributive; it was love for the community and its individual members. His love so wrapped the community that its warmth reached every individual.

[1] See pages 89ff.

God's love is also directed immediately to persons individually. He is concerned about their individual lives.

Because of that concern, He inspired the Prophets with moral instruction for individuals, and with instructions to rulers to care for individuals. It is part of the Prophets' function to warn individuals of the consequences of sin and to exhort them to repentance. 'Son of man, I have made thee a watchman unto the house of Israel; therefore hear the word at my mouth and give them warning from me' (Ezekiel 3: 17 and 33: 7). What the Prophets addressed to the house of Israel is instruction also to its members individually; it was actuated by God's love for them individually as well as for the people collectively.

It was also the Prophets' mission to bring a message of God's love directly to individuals. They were entrusted with both a law and gospel. 'The spirit of the Lord God is upon me; because the Lord hath anointed me to preach good tidings unto the meek; he hath sent me to bind up the broken hearted, to proclaim liberty to the captives, and the opening of the prison to them that are bound' (Isaiah 61: 1). So, too, Jeremiah's vision of the happier future includes the promise of divine grace for the distressed; 'For I have satiated the weary soul, and every sorrowful soul have I replenished' (Jeremiah 31: 25). Because the rulers of Israel neglected the welfare of their subjects, God Himself will care for them (Ezekiel 34). The unnamed author of Isaiah 57 puts in another way, and probably in different circumstances, the same belief in God's care for the individual. 'Thus saith the Lord: I dwell in the High and Holy place, but also with him who is of a contrite and humble spirit to revive the spirit of the humble and to revive the heart of the contrite ones' (Isaiah 57: 15). God cares for men. He is concerned for those who are poor in the economic sense and for those who are poor, distressed, in spirit. Such is God's love for men individually. It is embodied in the world order which is, throughout, His activity. Men are, therefore, individually involved in God's government of the universe. Their lives are dominated by it. Their individual fates must accord with it. It comprises both love and justice; it should, by its justice, bring men individually the consequences of their actions. But how can it be reconciled with justice that men's fortunes do not always correspond to their virtue? The idea of solidarity eased the problem but did not remove it.

The Prophets did not have a belief in an after life to enlarge the field in which the moral order could reveal its working. They could not extend its fulfilment to a life after death in which the apparent injustices of the earthly life will be redressed. The belief in an after-life with spiritual and moral significance came into Judaism later. The books of the Prophets do not present any clear evidence of it. They may, or may not, have shared the prevalent belief of their time that the dead continued a shadowy existence in an underworld. It would seem that men have always found it impossible to conceive either an end to their existence or its continuation to infinity. The Hebrews, like other ancient peoples, turned the dead into ghosts. In the superb poetry, though doubtful religion, of Isaiah 14, the writer describes the descent into the underworld of the Babylonian conqueror and the taunting welcome he received from the kings he conquered. But the Prophets do not make any use of a belief in an afterlife. Their thought did not go beyond this life and this world. The limitation adds grandeur to their spiritual and moral ideals.

In the Prophets' thought, therefore, the drama of human existence must reveal its plot, and significance, on earth. The day of judgment[1] would bring its denouement. It would come in the course of history to reveal fully the working of the moral order in human life. For humanity as a whole, and for nations, the limitation of human life to this world involved no difficulty. Nations live on, and their collective history will bring, soon or late, the appropriate consequences of their character and policies. The moral law in God's rule over the universe will fulfil itself in their lives and in the life of humanity. For individuals, the position was different; they might die before the day of judgment. But that difficulty did not, at first, arise for the Prophets. They believed and proclaimed that God's judgment was imminent; it would justify the righteous and condemn the wicked. This belief forms the context of most of the teaching of the Prophets, especially of the eigth century Prophets. A near day of judgment will vindicate the faith of the faithful, and bring punishment to the impious; it will establish for men a destiny corresponding to their deserts, bringing the fruits of righteousness to the righteous and the fruits of sin to the unrighteous. The 'day of the Lord' will redress the present apparent injustices. It will test the nations, but also individuals. 'Hear ye that are far off, what I have done: and, ye that are near, acknowledge my might. The sinners in Zion are afraid, trembling hath surprised the godless ones. Who among us shall dwell with the devouring fire? Who among us shall dwell with enduring (?intense) burnings?' (Isaiah 33: 13-14). The answer is, they who live righteously. The day of judgment will reveal the difference between them and the wicked. 'Then shall ye return and dis-

[1] See pages 152ff.

cern between the righteous and the wicked, between him that serveth God and him that serveth him not (Malachi 3: 18). When history again and again belied the Prophets' expectation, the day of judgment was put into the apocalyptic future. All would happen as they prognosticated 'in the end of days'. The problem of the fate of the individual grew in insistence, however, as the day of judgment was indefinitely postponed, until another world and another life were brought in to complete this world and this life. The final judgment on the lives of men, which was put into a larger context than life on earth, lighted up the truth in the Prophets' insistence on the connection between a man's relation to God and his attainment to the salvation which is fullness of life with God. But it may be said that, in the main, the absence of another life from the thought of the Prophets gives their teaching an heroic beauty.

The Prophets recognised that, while sin leads to suffering, not all suffering is caused by sin. It sometimes attends virtue. In an unrighteous world, the righteous may have to suffer for their righteousness, but their suffering may—nay, will—help the world to attain salvation. That is the general idea implied in the significance which the anonymous Prophet of the second part of the book of Isaiah gave to the suffering of Israel in exile. The pre-exilic Prophets had foretold that Israel would suffer destruction because of her sin. Their prophecy had come true; Judaea was conquered and devastated by Nebuchadrezzar, and its people were driven into exile. The suffering of exile was the punishment for sin. So Jeremiah and Ezekiel who witnessed it interpreted it.

A younger contemporary of Ezekiel, probably also living in Babylonia, the author of chapters 40 to 55 in the present book of Isaiah, accepted that interpretation for the past, but interpreted the present situation differently. He proclaimed, with the fervour of assured conviction, that the restoration of the exiles was at hand. Jeremiah and Ezekiel had prophesied that they would ultimately be restored. Deutero-Isaiah declared that they would be restored immediately. He based his prophecy on contemporary historic events. Cyrus, the Mede, had conquered Persia. Babylonia offered him an obvious lure for further conquest, with, because of its weakness, an assured prospect of victory. But the new imperial conqueror, unlike his Babylonian and Assyrian predecessors, did not disperse into exile the people he conquered; on the contrary, he cultivated their friendship by deference to their religions and nationalities. His policy, therefore, gave realistic ground for the expectation that he would permit, and even encourage, the Jewish exiles in Babylonia to return to their country. That expectation gave religious support to the Prophet's assurance that Cyrus would conquer Babylonia. In his faith it was God's will that the exiles should return so that Israel might fulfil its function as God's witness. Cyrus was His servant, His Messiah, anointed—that is, appointed—by Him to carry out His purpose. The glad prospect must mean that Israel's sin has been forgiven. 'Comfort ye, comfort ye my people, saith your God. Speak ye comfortably to Jerusalem and cry unto her that her tribulation is accomplished, that her iniquity is pardoned; that she hath received of the Lord's hand double for all her sins' (Isaiah 40: 1-2).

But Israel's sin could not fully explain its suffering. It must have had a purpose. For, after all, the Jews were no less righteous than the Babylonians. Moreover, the exile must have grieved the pious ones to a special degree because of their piety; and it may well be that their fellow exiles in Babylonia treated their piety with contumely. Sin could not explain their misery. Deutero-Isaiah, therefore, gives another explanation of Israel's suffering in four poems about a suffering servant of God (Isaiah 42: 1-4, 49: 1-6, 50: 4-9, 52: 13 to 53: 12). Scholars do not interpret these poems with anything near unanimity, except to reject the theological view which found in them a description of a future Messiah. Some say that the poems were intended to describe the ideal individual; others that the life of Jeremiah, or of some other prophet, inspired them. Still others maintain that the poems were intended to explain the suffering of the pious section of Jews; and, finally, others think that the author wanted to explain the suffering of the actual Israel by reference to the ideal Israel.

It would go beyond the scope of this book to discuss the problem in its details or the arguments for the diverse solutions. But it seems to the present writer that the following suggestion meets most of the difficulties the poems present, and goes a long way to reconciling the various interpretations.

They are a parable to point the moral that the service of God may entail suffering. The fact that the author does not indicate their parabolic character does not argue against the suggestion. The Prophets did not always mark the change from their statements to the parables illustrating them. The book of Jonah is an outstanding example, a parable told as history; the story of the unfaithful wife in Hosea may be another. If this suggestion is valid, then the poems gave an explanation at the same time for the suffering of the Jews in exile and for the suffering of the pious ones among them. Their case is like that of a prophet who had to endure ignominy, pain and martyrdom. But by his suffering he fulfilled his purpose, for by his life and death, he 'justified many'—that is, made them realise their sinfulness, so that they said—'they' meaning just people indefinitely—that because of the human situation he had to suffer to impress his instruction on others. In that way he promoted the true religion which leads to salvation.

The poems may have been based on the life of Jeremiah, but in their present context they need not be referred to any historic, or even ideal, individual. Deutero-Isaiah says, in the use he makes of them: The position of the Jews is like that of a prophet who had to undergo, in connection with his service of God, suffering and death, and through them attained his aim.

Whether he had in mind the actual Israel, the ideal Israel, or the pious section of the actual Israel, does not matter; the idea remains the same, that, because of the moral condition of the world, suffering attends the highest service of God; and it serves to bring men to recognise and worship Him.

Jeremiah discovered the same idea through his experience. When, in a colloquy with God, he complained that he suffered through serving Him, while those who opposed Him lived happily, the only answer he could find was that he must be prepared for even greater hardship in carrying out his mission. 'Righteous art thou, O Lord, when I plead with thee: yet I would reason the cause with thee; wherefore doth the way of the wicked prosper? wherefore are all they at ease that deal very treacherously? Thou hast planted them, yea, they have taken root; they grow, yea, they bring forth fruit; thou art near in their mouth, and far from their heart. . . . But thou, O Lord, knowest me; thou seest me and triest mine heart towards thee'. He gets the answer: 'If thou hast run with the footmen, and they have wearied thee, then how canst thou contend with horses? and though in a land of peace thou art secure, yet how wilt thou do in the pride of Jordan?' (Jeremiah 12: 1-2, 3a and 5). The answer means that the prophetic mission will bring him still greater hardship. But he has the confident faith that God will support and strengthen him if he remains faithful to it (Jeremiah 15: 19ff).

The idea emerges from the poems of the suffering servant and from Jeremiah's interpretation of his suffering that individuals sometimes suffer because of the sins of others. The apparent inconsistency between the doctrine that suffering attends sin and the realisation that it may be a concomitant of the highest service of God is removed by recognising that in the second case it is also caused by sin, the sin of others, and that in both cases it has a reformative purpose; in the first case, to induce repentance in those who suffer, in the second case, to influence others to repent. The answer, however, which the Prophets gave to those who questioned God's rule insisted that sin must lead to destruction. The fact that human life did not at present show a connection between righteousness and happiness on the one hand, and on the other between unrighteousness and misery, was irrevelant. The future will prove their doctrine. The existing violations of God's law of righteousness will soon or ultimately reveal their evil consequences. The threats of the coming judgment all amount to the ultimate argument: You will see God's rule.

The arguments which the Prophets used to prove God's activity in human life were for the irreligious.

For themselves, they knew that they who serve God have in their relation with Him the fulfilment of their lives. To possess God is all that matters. The faith which filled and upheld them is expressed by the Psalmist: 'Whom have I in heaven but thee? and there is none upon earth that I desire besides thee. My flesh and my heart faileth; but God is the strength of my heart and my portion for ever'. (Psalm 73: 25-26). So Jeremiah, in spite of his suffering, finds a joy in his prophetic calling which transcends its pain. But the doctrine that 'to know God' is the highest attainment of man and the greatest good in human life could not overcome the irreligion that denied the activity of God in human life. That activity can be perceived only spiritually; only by a capacity to apprehend spiritual realities. The Prophets themselves saw that activity in the whole universal order, in nature, in human history, in the fortunes and misfortunes of individuals. But it requires spiritual apprehension to see God in the universe and in human life.

It is the inherent problem of religion that it requires what it tries to give. The appreciation of spiritual values requires spiritual capacity. The lack of it, as Isaiah complained, is the root trouble in the human situation. God can be seen only by His own light. That is why the movement from irreligion to religion is often through conversion, a sudden radical change in personality and outlook; but the movement from some spiritual apprehension to complete faith in God can be a progressive process. God can come flooding in, even through small openings, but He may also enter a human life by stages corresponding to its spiritual growth. But inevitably the arguments for religion have to be drawn from religion. Against the irreligion which denied God's activity in human affairs, the

Prophets could only affirm that they saw it in the whole course of human history and of human lives; that He was not a God 'afar off but not near'. But it requires faith in God to discern His activity, as to feel His presence.

ELEVEN

THE HUMAN PROBLEM

THE Prophets' treatment of human suffering does not solve, but only eases, the problem it poses for theism. Not all suffering appears to be caused by sin, whether the sin of those who suffer or of others. The fact is that suffering did not present a problem in the thought of the Prophets. Because of their realistic and comprehensive theism, they did not see in it a challenge to faith in God. Since it occurs in the world which is under His rule, it must accord with His will, and what accords with His will must be just and good. Therefore a Prophet refuting Persian dualism quotes God: 'I am the Lord, and there is none else. I form the light and create darkness; I make well-being and ill-being: I the Lord do all these things' (Isaiah 45: 6f). This attitude to suffering was more than submission to God's will; it emptied suffering of its evil, and, therefore, of its need for special justification in theistic belief. Uncompromising monotheism must assign to all that exists a place in God's scheme, and the quality of partaking in His goodness. Habakkuk sums up the general view of the Prophets when he says that faith must triumph over suffering. Suffering was for them not a religious problem because their thought was theocentric, not anthropocentric; they did not feel it necessary to justify the ways of God to men but to bring the ways of men into accord with the will of God.

In later Judaism suffering was given the power of atonement, so that Israel's suffering was called the 'chastisements of love'—God's love. But there is no hint of this doctrine in the thought of the Prophets. They ascribed a reformative power to the suffering caused by sin. It would stimulate repentance. And they complained that all the experiences of the past which should have taught the people to repent have not roused them to realise their spiritual need (Amos 4: 6-11, Zechariah 1: 4). They seem to have missed a common fact of human experience. Suffering does not always generate repentance, it sometimes hardens the heart against God. Some react to it like Job's wife (Job 2: 9). It requires faith to transmute hard experience into spiritual enrichment. And it must be the faith which in its appreciation of spiritual values rises above all material or physical tests, the faith which equates the highest good with devotion to God. The Prophets themselves had a faith so deep and mighty that, though it could be pained, it could not be shaken or challenged by suffering. They thought that if all men were guided by such a faith, evil would be eliminated from human life and good established. And they believed that men would be brought to it by suffering the consequences of sin.

That view of the power of suffering differs from the belief that it has the power of atonement in the usual theological meaning of atonement. Though that belief is sometimes found in later Judaism, the theological doctrine, developed in its fullness outside Judaism, that suffering is a universal necessity to atone for sin implied, or was based on, two assumptions: (1) that all men were by nature laden with sin and (2) that physical suffering had an inherent spiritual potency. Both these ideas were not in the Prophets' thought.

They recognised that sin prevailed but they did not believe that it was natural, let alone inevitable. They did not believe that suffering, but that repentance, could establish the relation with God.

The Prophets' acceptance of suffering did not imply indifference to it. They were pained by the suffering they witnessed, and grieved by their own prognostications of woe and destruction. 'I am pained at my very heart; my heart is disquieted in me; I cannot hold my peace; because thou hast heard, O my soul, the sound of the trumpet, the alarm of war. Destruction upon destruction is cried, for the whole land is spoiled. . . . How long shall I see the standard (of war), and hear the sound of the trumpet?' (Jeremiah 4: 19-21). 'Thus saith the Lord: A voice is heard in Ramah, lamentation, and bitter weeping, Rachel weeping for her children; she refuseth to be comforted for her children, because they are not' (Jeremiah 31: 15). And because of their sense of complete identification with God, they ascribe their feelings to Him. That is the way He feels. Even when men suffer, as they must, for their sins, God grieves for them and longs for their repentance to avert the suffering.

But why do men sin? They choose to do so. That is implied in all the exhortations of the Prophets. Men are so constituted that they have the power, and feel the desire, to sin. That is probably the vague idea behind the complaint which a Prophet puts into the mouth of Jews who were suffering distress. 'O Lord why dost thou make us to err from thy ways, and hardenest our heart from thy fear?' (Isaiah 63: 17). The complaint would be an accusation in a system of thought that conceived God's rule in terms of specific edicts, but when that rule is conceived in terms of law, the complaint amounts to the question, why, in the divine order of the universe, has man been endowed with power to sin and burdened with the inclination to it? The Prophets do not answer that question. Again, they accept as right and good what God has ordained.

They have two general ideas about sin. The first is that it is a disease of the heart, a perversion of the inner life, a corruption of the spirit, which men produce in themselves. God does not prevent them. They resolved the obvious paradox, that in a world under the absolute and universal sovereignty of God men could defy His will, by a daring assumption, which at first sight seems only to shift, but not to remove, the difficulty. Man, they said, is responsible for sin, but God gives him the power to sin. The connection thus made between God's rule and man's sin must be understood in the light of the Prophets' theistic realism. Obviously men sin. That fact can be reconciled with God's complete and universally comprehensive sovereignty by the inference that He allows men to sin.

There could be no escape from the problem created by the existence of sin through belief in a power of evil separate from God. The later Jewish doctrine that 'two powers' was the arch-heresy against monotheism, was in line with the Prophets' thought. Satan, in the Old Testament, is not an independent power of evil, but a mean angel who brings before God accusations against men. Sin could not be taken out of God's rule. But at the same time the blame for sin lies not on Him but on the sinners. The involved inconsistency must ever haunt theism. The Prophets seem to go further than the doctrine that God made men 'sufficient to stand but free to fall'. They added that He gives them the power to sin, which can only mean that He supports them in the use of their freedom, even when they exercise it in defiance of Him. It is a daring doctrine, and impressive. God values human freedom above His loathing for sin. The doctrine is toned down when put negatively. Men's sin, which breaks or strains their relation with God, shuts them out from the help which God, in His grace, gives them when they try to make the most of their lives. 'Behold, the Lord's hand is not shortened, that it cannot save, neither his ear heavy, that it cannot hear; but your iniquities have separated between you and your God, and your sins have hid his face from you, that he will not hear' (Isaiah 59: 1-2). But sin does not deprive men of the power to will and act, which God confers on them through His activity in human life. Men's constant moral freedom is clearly implied in all the teaching of the Prophets. They can always choose to do what is right.

Even if men yield to their tendency to sin, their sinfulness does not inexorably control their destiny, they can repent. That is the Prophets' other general idea about sin. Its consequences are not immutably fixed, they can be averted by repentance. Though the human situation may become desperate, as Jeremiah thought in his despair, it can be remedied. Hence the Prophets, while painting the situation in darkest colours, call insistently and passionately for repentance. The divine order in the universe embodies in its righteousness love and justice. All the love works for repentance. God's love is not killed by men's sin. He is urgent to save sinners; He longs for their repentance. 'Therefore say thou unto them, Thus saith the Lord of Hosts, Return unto me, and I will return unto you' (Zechariah 1: 3). 'O Jerusalem, wash thine heart from wickedness, that thou mayest be saved. How long shall thine evil thoughts lodge with thee?' (Jeremiah 4: 14). God does not let men pursue evil without warning them of its consequences. That is the Prophet's function (Amos 3: 7, Jeremiah 11: 6ff; Ezekiel 33). God longs to deliver the sinful, but He cannot unless they turn to Him. If they do turn to Him, the wicked forsaking his way, and the unrighteous man his thoughts: He will have mercy upon them and abundantly pardon (Isaiah 55: 6f). God hates sin but not the sinful.

The human situation is accepted. Man is so constituted that he is prone to sin. But this tendency does not deprive him of his freedom to choose his course of life. God's moral order gives men freedom to effect in themselves a change of heart, a conversion at the centre of personality which would alter their relation to Him. Men need, with a tragic urgency, such a radical change—conversion through repentance. The repentance will both express and produce the conversion. Dedicate yourselves to God, pleads Jeremiah, and put away the impurity of your hearts, men of Judah and dwellers in Jerusalem. In the preceding verse he makes the same plea with a different metaphor. 'Break up your fallow ground and do not sow among thorns' (Jeremiah 4: 3f). Cleanse yourselves inwardly to merit the fruits of repentance. So, too, Hosea, adopting the same metaphor as Jeremiah, pleads for the inward change which will bring the full fruition of a right relation with God. 'Sow yourselves with righteousness, reap according to piety, break up the fallow ground, for it is time to seek the Lord until he come and rain righteousness (i.e., the fullness of virtue in his sight) on you (teach you righteousness)' (Hosea 10: 12). Ezekiel makes the same plea. 'Cast away from you all your transgressions, wherein ye have transgressed and make you a new heart and a new spirit' (Ezekiel 18: 31). A new heart and a new spirit, a heart in its wholeness and a mind in its singleness devoted to God, the whole personality infused with faith in Him. And when men strive for a new heart and new spirit, God will confirm their striving. His rule assures the efficacy of sincere repentance.[1]

It is, however, the tragedy in the human situation that sin prevents repentance. The sinful heart cannot realise its evil condition and feel the urgent need to change it. In his softer moods, Jeremiah feels the tragedy. 'O Lord, I know that the way of man is not in himself; it is not in man that walketh to direct his steps' (Jeremiah 10: 23). Not because he has no freedom but because he has enslaved himself to sin. Sin has corrupted his heart, that is, his spirit, his inner life. 'Ye walk every one after the stubbornness of his evil heart, so that ye hearken not unto me' (Jeremiah 16: 12). And the heart cannot be trusted. 'The heart is deceitful above all things, and it is desperately sick; who can know it?' (Jeremiah 17: 9). The sin of Judah is engraved deeply and firmly in their heart (Jeremiah 17: 1); their idolatry is both within them and constantly with them (Ezekiel 14: 3) where the law of God should be (Deuteronomy 6: 6 and 8). Just as true religion lives within man, being spiritual attainment, so sin, being spiritual failure, is inner corruption. 'Their doings will not suffer them to turn unto their God; for the spirit of whoredom is within them, and they know not the Lord' (Hosea 5: 4). Sin is not merely doing wrong, it is being wrong. Because sin is so deeply ingrained, the situation is desperate. 'Can the Ethiopian change his skin, or the leopard his spots: then may ye also do good, who are accustomed to do evil' (Jeremiah 13: 23).

Yet there is a chance, otherwise the Prophets' exhor-

[1] See page 48.

tations and pleadings would have had no sense. Though the sin is ingrained it can be overcome. Men always have the power to repent. They are not corrupt by nature; on the contrary, they are inherently capable of attaining the highest good. To know God is as natural for man as for the ox to know his master (Isaiah 1: 3). Men know instinctively the right way to live. Religion, in its spiritual and moral demands, offers them the way of true self-expression. When they choose to sin, they violate their true nature. Their self-corruption, not their natural endowment, causes them to forsake God. 'The stork in the heaven knoweth her appointed times; and the turtle and the swallow and the crane observe the time of their coming; but My people know not the ordinance of the Lord' (Jeremiah 8: 7). Though the religious attitude naturally belongs to human nature, men wilfully destroy it in themselves. They forget God, though all nature reveals Him. 'Declare ye this in the house of Jacob, and publish it in Judah, saying, Hear now this, O foolish people and without understanding; who have eyes and see not; who have ears, and hear not; Fear ye not me? saith the Lord; will ye not tremble at my presence, who has placed the sand for the bound of the sea, by a perpetual decree, that it cannot pass it? And though the waves thereof toss themselves, yet can they not prevail; though they roar, yet can they not pass over it. But this people have a revolting and rebellious heart; they are revolted and gone. Neither say they in their heart, Let us now fear the Lord our God, who giveth rain, both the former and the latter, in its season, who reserveth unto us the appointed weeks of the harvest' (Jeremiah 5: 20-24). Indifference to God, which is the root disease in the human situation, is unnatural for men.

The conception of man implied in the thought of

the Prophets combines a high estimation of what he is naturally and a very low estimation of what he is actually. His potentiality far exceeds his condition. The ideal man is for the Prophets also the natural man; God makes men an image of Himself. They would have subscribed to an old Jewish prayer which declares: The soul which Thou hast given me is pure. In spite of their severe strictures on men and their conduct, the Prophets conceived of man as naturally moral. But the actual man has corrupted his proper nature by sin, not through any necessity in his nature but through his wilful choice, with the result that the human situation has become so desperate that it can be saved only by a radical change, through repentance, which will bring men into the grace of God. And they will repent. 'Shall men fall and not rise up again? shall one turn away and not return?' (Jeremiah 8: 4).

The pained insistence in the Prophets' exhortation to repentance was actuated by a sense of urgency. The day of judgment was near. 'And because I will do this unto thee, prepare to meet thy God, O Israel' (Amos 4: 12). 'It may be that the house of Judah will hear all the evil which I purpose to do unto them; that they may return every man from his evil way; that I may forgive their iniquity and their sin' (Jeremiah 36: 3). 'Thus saith the Lord, Keep ye judgment, and do righteousness, for my salvation is near to come, and my righteousness to be revealed' (Isaiah 56: 1).

Logically the conclusion should have been that there is no hope for sinners who do not repent. And sometimes the Prophets adopt that conclusion; Jeremiah expresses it bitterly in his harshest mood when the spiritual heedlessness of the people bore his spirit down with discouragement to the darkest despair. But even he could not give up all hope; his faith kept it alive. 'Return, thou backsliding Israel, said the Lord; I will not look in anger upon you, for I am merciful, said the Lord' (Jeremiah 3: 12). He sometimes despaired of men but never of God's mercy; faith in God sustained his hope. The Prophet drew from it the assurance that men will, must, soon or late, turn to God. God's grace assures ultimately regenerate men.

Faith in God must prevent complete despair of men. Their essential nature, conferred on them by God, will not permit them to abide permanently in sin. Being His children, they will be compelled ultimately to turn to the Father. The two lines of thought, that men's nature will drive them to God, and that God in His grace will revive them spiritually, are interwoven in the Prophets' hope for the future. Sinners will realise their need for God. 'Come and let us return unto the Lord, for he hath torn, and he will heal us; he hath smitten, and he will bind us up' (Hosea 6: 1). 'And I will give them one heart and one way, that they may fear me for ever; for the good of them, and of their children after them' (Jeremiah 32: 39 cf. 24: 7). Ezekiel expressed the same confident hope. 'A new heart also will I give you, and a new spirit will I put within you: and I will take away the stony heart out of your flesh, and I will give you an heart of flesh. And I will put my spirit within you, and cause you to walk in my statutes, and ye shall keep my judgments, and do them' (Ezekiel 36: 26f).

It is inconceivable that a world under the rule of God should succumb completely to the power of sin. It will be saved from such a disaster; God himself will save it. 'And he saw that there was no man, and wondered that there was no intercessor; therefore his own arm brought salvation unto him, and his righteousness, it upheld him' (Isaiah 59: 16 cf. 63: 5). In the end sin must be conquered because it is incompatible with the rule of God. God will, by wooing sinners as a lover woos his beloved, coax them on the way to overcome it. 'I will allure her, and bring her unto the wilderness and speak to her heart' (Hosea 2: 14). And He will be patient with them until they do turn to Him in repentance. 'And, therefore, will the Lord wait, that he may be gracious unto you, and, therefore, will he be exalted, that he may have mercy upon you; for the Lord is a God of judgment; blessed are all they that wait for him' (Isaiah 30: 18). God alone is the saviour. 'Thou, O Lord, art our father; our redeemer from everlasting is thy name' (Isaiah 63: 16). Sinners, as the next verse implies, may ask Him for deliverance. Whatever be the historic situation which evoked this prayer, its spirit conforms with the attitude of the Prophets. It accords with the loving nature of God to help sinners to repent.

God's sovereignty ensures that in the end the moral order in the universe will overcome sin. God's grace will assert itself and men will respond to it. The ultimate salvation of men is assured by His rule, and His love will rejoice when it is attained. The freedom of men is, thus, after all, restricted by the sovereignty of God, but the restriction belongs to the true nature of man. Because God loathes sin, men, His children, cannot permanently rest in it. The human situation will be changed. There will be a new world. Both sin and suffering will be eliminated. Death, too, will be destroyed. 'He hath swallowed up death for ever; and the Lord God will wipe away tears from off all faces; and the reproach of his people shall he take from off all the earth; for the Lord hath spoken it' (Isaiah 25: 8). The ultimate future will bring the solution of the human problem.

TWELVE

THE MEANING OF HISTORY

It follows logically from the Prophets' conception of God and His activity in human life, that human history is under His rule, and it must, therefore, make moral sense. So the Prophets' thought includes a philosophy of history which interprets its course and predicts its ultimate issue. They do not expound it but it is clearly expressed in their judgments on contemporaneous events, in their prognostications of future events, and in their hopes for the ultimate consummation of the history of mankind. It takes into its scope all the nations. The Prophets' belief in a universal God enforced on them, as His spokesmen, a concern about the condition and fate of all mankind. Jeremiah felt in his call the commission to be 'a prophet to the nations'. In the allegory in the Book of Jonah God sends a Jewish prophet to urge the people of Nineveh to repent that their city might be saved. The author of the second part of the Book of Isaiah addresses to all nations a call to worship God (Isaiah 41:1ff, 49:1ff, 51:4ff), and all mankind is involved in his doctrine of Israel's mission to be 'a light to the nations'.

The prophecies against, or about, the nations included in nearly all the books of the prophets are not merely casual additions, they belong integrally to the framework of prophecy. Not only the history of the Hebrews but the history of all nations comes under God's sovereignty. 'Are ye not as the children of Ethiopians unto me, O children of Israel? saith the

Lord. Have not I brought up Israel out of the land of Egypt, and the Philistines from Caphtor, and the Syrians from Kir?' (Amos 9: 7). The prophet wanted in the first place to refute the belief in a national god. The God from whom he brought a message ruled all the nations, just as He ruled the whole universe. And He judges the conduct of all nations. Sometimes the Prophets predict disaster for a nation because of its treatment of, or attitude to, the Jews, but more often they attribute a nation's misfortunes to its overweening pride, idolatry, or general unrighteousness (Amos 1: 3ff, Nahum 3: 4 and 9, Isaiah 10: 5ff, 23: 9 and 37: 26). They feel a sympathy for the nations while predicting their fate (Isaiah 15: 5, 16: 4, 9 and 11, 21: 2-4, cf. Book of Jonah). But all the nations must be spiritually and morally purged.

The Prophets knew specifically only the nations of the limited world which included little more than the lands covered now by the term Middle East; though they realised that the world was larger. They may have known the names of some distant lands, but generally they refer vaguely to distant lands as the 'isles from afar'. These references support the inference from their prophecies about the nations that they meant to cover the whole world of man with their philosophy of history.

Three principles emerge, in that philosophy, from the fundamental idea that human history is under the direction of God.

(1) The first is that the moral law governs history, so that a nation's history conforms to its moral character. Righteousness establishes its well-being, unrighteousness brings misfortune. This principle did not always fit actual events. When Assyria conquered Palestine, Isaiah explained that God used her as His instrument

to bring on the Hebrews the consequence of their disloyalty to Him. The explanation had, however, an obvious weakness; it explained the Hebrews' misfortune, it did not explain the Assyrians' good fortune, for were they any better than the Hebrews? But, Isaiah adds, Assyria, too, will be punished for her overweening pride in thinking that she gained her victories by her own strength, not realising that they were given her by God to carry out His purposes. 'Wherefore it shall come to pass, that when the Lord hath performed his whole work upon Mount Zion and on Jerusalem I will punish the fruit of the stout heart of the king of Assyria, and the glory of his high looks. For he hath said, By the strength of my hand I have done it, and by my wisdom, . . . Shall the axe boast itself against him that heweth therewith? Shall the saw magnify itself against him that moveth it? As if a rod should shake them that lift it up, or as if a staff should lift up him that is not wood' (Isaiah 10: 12f and 15 cf. Isaiah 36: 26f). God employs human instruments—that is His way—in His rule over human life, using, for His righteous ends, even those who themselves are unrighteous.

Zechariah gives another reason for the punishment that will overtake the nations which have afflicted the Jews. True, God used them to impress on the Jews the consequences of their sin, but they went too far, exceeding their commission (Zechariah 1: 15). The author of the later Pseudepigraphical Book of Enoch expresses a similar idea (Enoch 89: 59 and 90: 20-27).

The seeming paradox, that God gives success for a time to a nation which does not morally deserve it, is an inevitable corollary of the belief that God rules human history. It happens; so it must accord with the divine government of humanity's life; and such events must be faced with faith; as Habakkuk did when, painfully puzzled by the success and cruelty of the Chaldeans, he rose above the challenge to his faith by exercising it.

History has on more than one occasion given support to the Prophets' belief that God uses an unrighteous nation to enforce on other nations the consequences of their unrighteousness. The wicked draw their strength from the lack of righteousness in others, just as disease germs feed on physical frailty. Totalitarianism has grown out of the social shortcomings of the democracies. At the same time, history has justified the faith that foresees the ultimate defeat of unrighteousness even at the time of its apparent success; though it has not always verified empirically the belief in the victory of the righteous.

The theist, following the logic of theism, must attach paramount power to spiritual and moral factors in directing the course of human history. This is what the Prophets' philosophy of history affirms. It can meet the challenge of the materialistic philosophy of history by pointing to the historic fact that prosperity has not made a nation strong, nor has physical power saved it from destruction. The moral degeneration in the Roman Empire is given by historians a decisive place among the causes that destroyed it. A lack of righteousness rotted it even before it fell. The Prophets' predictions that the low spiritual and moral conditions in the Hebrew kingdoms would lead to their destruction were fulfilled. Other examples could be adduced from history to support the negative aspect of the Prophets' philosophy of history, that national unrighteousness brings national ruin. The positive affirmation of that philosophy, that righteousness gives a nation unconquerable strength, has yet to be tested fully. But history has produced some, and produces increasing, evidence of its truth.

Moreover, God's rule cannot be seen in isolated events but in the whole course of history. True, the Prophets did occasionally refer to some special event, like the exodus from Egypt, as evidence of God's rule over human history. So, too, they used the crises in their time, to support, or to impress, their doctrine. Their prophecies of doom were often evoked by an existing crisis or by one which they thought to be imminent. The reports of a vast Scythian host from the North moving southward, invading, plundering and spreading destruction and death on its way, prompted Jeremiah to foretell the impending destruction of Judah in punishment for its sins and to urge repentance to avert the threatening calamity. When the invading host by-passed Judaea, his prophetic credibility was—naturally—impugned, but he was certain that the escape was only a respite to allow more time for repentance; the judgment was sure. Such references to single events were intended, however, only to light up the whole course of history, which is in its totality the work of God, with its every detail fitting into a plan comprehending all time. The Prophets addressed themselves to the contemporary situation but they interpreted it in the context of the historical process. They rise above history to see the meaning of its events, with a vision that reaches beyond the present to apprehend its relation to the ultimate future; so that the main proof for the Prophets' philosophy of history must be found in the whole course of a people's history, lighted up by its crises.

(2) The second principle, or affirmation, in the Prophets' philosophy of history is that there will be a day of judgment which will bring to men and nations

the consequences of their righteousness or lack of it. Whoever said 'World history is a world judgment' was anticipated by the Prophets. The epigram sums up this aspect of their philosophy of history. It follows as a corollary from their belief in the domination of the moral law. Men and nations will be judged for the moral quality of their lives.

There was a popular belief in the coming of a 'day of God', originally, it would seem, with the expectation that it would bring the lasting happiness men wanted. The belief probably originated in the congenital tendency among men to project into the future what they miss in the present. The Prophets gave the belief a different content; the day of God would have an opposite character from what the people wished, and expected, in their easy-going religion. 'Woe unto you that desire the day of the Lord! wherefore would ye have the day of the Lord? It is darkness, and not light' (Amos 5: 18). It will be a day of judgment, because the unrighteous conditions in the world called for a judgment. God cannot be mocked. The moral order cannot be violated with impunity. Unrighteousness must be purged out by its consequences. The prophet who prophesies smooth things is a false prophet. How could he, if he were truly inspired by God, prophesy that all will be well when all is morally so ill? 'The day of God', when He would manifest the fullness of His rule over the world, could not be 'a good time', because the world did not deserve it. The contrast between the world as it is and the world as it ought to be generated the Prophets' certainty about the coming of a day of judgment. The world cannot, under God, endure as it is. It had to be set right. But that could not happen without drastic changes which only a hard, grim and terrible experience could produce by bringing home to men the consequences of their sin.

There is considerable ambiguity about the time of the day of judgment. Sometimes it is put in the immediate future and sometimes in a remote and undefined future. It is not always possible to decide which is meant. The vagueness conforms to the Prophets' philosophy of history. On the one hand, the judgment must come; on the other hand every crisis could be interpreted as a judgment. When, therefore, the Prophets proclaim that the day of God is near (Isaiah 13:6, Ezekiel 7:7, 30: 3, Zephaniah 1:7 and 14), they may refer to an impending event with crucial historic importance, or they may mean that the apocalyptic day of final judgment is near, identifying it, at times, with an imminent crisis, and referring it, at other times, to a vague future with an imminent event as its prototype. The alternatives bring out the fact that the Prophets did not separate history and apocalypse.

The final judgment, whether immediate or remote, is for the Prophets a fact of history. They describe it with apocalyptic exaggeration, but it will come within, not beyond, the process of history. They interpreted history with the eschatology of apocalyptic, but their apocalyptic did not supersede history. God's purposes for mankind will be fulfilled within it. History will bring the final judgment.

In their use of 'the day of judgment', the Prophets, therefore, combined history and apocalypse. Apocalypse is not only the long view, looking beyond immediate events, but also the deeper view, interpreting them. It reveals the ultimate meaning of history, but the meaning flashes in each historic crisis. Later apocalyptic literature put the day of judgment into an ultimate future; the Prophets give it also an historic immediacy; it is both near and far. A Prophet may identify it with an event which he thinks imminent in his own time, but he gives the event ultimate significance. Or he may think of an ultimate event, and see its prototype in an immediate one. When the Prophets' references to events that involve a day of judgment are translated into a philosophy of history, their general thesis seems to be that an imminent crisis or calamity is a testing time; it may be the apocalyptic day of judgment, but it may also differ in that history will afterwards continue its course to a final consummation. The prediction of a final judgment is so often identified with an immediate crisis that they cannot be disentangled. The important idea is that the day of judgment belongs to history. There is, for example, no knowing with certainty whom Ezekiel intended by Gog and Magog, but it may reasonably, and perhaps even safely, be conjectured that he meant nations or empires on the plane of history. With the constant wars and threats of war that pervaded the Prophets' world, it was natural for them to expect a climacteric war to initiate, or effect, the judgment.

In the later apocalyptic literature, which, partly issued out of the Prophets' unfulfilled hopes and promises, the day of judgment assumed increasingly supernatural features. The Prophets' figurative language became literal in the later apocalypses, which, unlike the Prophets, leave the realities of earth for dreams of heaven. In the Prophets' thought the final judgment was not a supernatural event but an event in history. For them apocalypse was not transcendental history, but history was apocalypse actualised.

The Prophets' apocalyptic treatment of history explains why they added prophecies of hope to their prognostications of doom; the combination belongs to eschatology. A bright future will follow the darkness of the judgment (e.g. Isaiah, Chapters 3 and 4). It is stated explicitly and briefly by Jeremiah: 'That day is great, so that none is like it; it is even the time of Jacob's trouble, but he shall be saved out of it' (Jeremiah 30: 7). So Jeremiah's book, heavy with gloomy forebodings, yet contains the brightest hope for the spiritual future (Chapters 30-33). The apocalyptic framework in which the Prophets put history enabled them, perhaps compelled is the more appropriate verb, to combine predictions of doom with prophecies of hope. At any rate, the contrast between the two cannot be used as an argument that they are by different authors. In some cases that conclusion may be enforced by other considerations. But the Prophets' philosophy of history needs the combination.

The final judgment will bring a permanent purification. 'I will turn my hand upon thee, and thoroughly purge away thy dross, and will take away all thy tin; and I will restore thy judges as at the first, and thy counsellors as at the beginning, afterward thou shalt be called the city of righteousness, the faithful city' (Isaiah 1: 25-26). 'And it shall come to pass, that he that is left in Zion, and he that remaineth in Jerusalem, shall be called holy, even every one that is written among the living in Jerusalem; when the Lord shall have washed away the filth of the daughters of Zion, and shall have purged the blood of Jerusalem from the midst thereof, by the spirit of judgment and by the spirit of burning'[1] (Isaiah 4: 3-4). 'But who may abide the day of his coming? and who shall stand when he appeareth? for he is like a refiner's fire, and like fullers' soap' (Malachi 3: 2).

[1] Does this mean purging as by fire?

Did the Prophets think that the doom which they predicted would be averted? The answer cannot be given with any approximation to certainty. Scholars differ about it. Plenty of evidence can be adduced to support both positive and negative answers. That fact proves that neither is comprehensively valid. The divergences in the Prophets' statements which bear on the question may be reconciled in one of three ways. (i) The doom would be averted if men repent, but being hardened in sin, they will not repent, so that the doom in the judgment is inevitable. (ii) The moods of the same Prophet change between hope and despair, or different prophets are dominated by different moods. (iii) The judgment must pronounce a general doom but the righteous and those who repent will be saved. The third possible explanation fits the general apocalyptic thesis: 'Repent for the Kingdom of God is at hand', which is the same as 'Repent for my righteousness is near' (Isaiah 56: 1).

The consequences of sin should serve, in God's ordering of the universe, to produce repentance. Their purpose as punishments is disciplinary and reformative. The idea pervades all the preaching of the Prophets that the misfortunes resulting from sin should produce repentance. But in their stubbornness men refuse to heed the warnings of the Prophets or the moral admonition of experience. So they will bring on themselves the final judgment which, in God's purpose, will enforce the purification required to bring the world under His rule. He will overrule the sinfulness of humanity. That tremendous, and perhaps even startling, affirmation follows inevitably from the central thought of the Prophets.

(3) The third element in the Prophets' philosophy is their Messianic hope. It springs directly from their

monotheism. Their vision of the ultimate future, 'the end of days', issues from the first verse of the Bible. The belief that God is the Creator of the world compelled the confident belief that He will finally bring it into full conformity with His nature. Its condition must come to represent faithfully the nature of its Creator by obedience to His law. The rule of God must be justified by history, and fulfilled in its ultimate consummation.

The Messianism of the Prophets is a very simple doctrine. The world will be cleansed of its evil and good will be finally established for ever. Social injustices will be eliminated from the life of mankind and human societies will be infused with justice and love. War, and preparations for it, will be abolished; peace will cover the earth under the rule of righteousness. Some of the Messianic prophecies begin with, or include, the reign of an ideal king. The description Messianic for the ultimate future of mankind is derived from them. The king was called Messiah (in Greek, *Christos*), which means literally anointed, and signified appointed by God. The ideal king would be a Messiah in the sense in which all the kings of the Hebrews were. He would be an ordinary human being, descended from David whose dynasty maintained permanent rule over Judaea, but perfect in devotion to God and ruling according to His law. But the ideal king, when he is mentioned, is only one element in the Messianic picture.

The Messianic consummation will be rooted in the universal worship of the true God. So the Prophets' description of the perfected world which is the goal of the historic process gives the central, the fundamental, and the paramount, place to the universal and effective belief in God. 'They shall not hurt nor destroy in all my holy mountain for the earth shall be full of the knowledge of the Lord as the waters cover the sea' (Isaiah 11: 9)—concludes one Prophet's vision of the future. Jeremiah's prophecy of the new covenant, when 'they shall all know me from the least of them to the greatest of them' means the same thing; and so do Ezekiel's 'new spirit and new heart', and Joel's prediction about the universal outpouring of divine inspiration (Joel 2: 28f). All mankind (all men) shall look to God (Isaiah 17: 7).

The author of Isaiah 11 extends the Messianic picture to include physical nature. Harmony will prevail in it. The Prophets use nature not only to supply figures and analogies for their instruction about human life, but also and even more so, to testify to the power and goodness of God. The problem raised by the things in it which are ugly, cruel, or affect men's lives adversely was partly overcome by the Messianic hope which envisaged a time when the conflicting elements in it will be harmonised. Because God's rule covers the whole of creation, the physical world must ultimately attain perfection (cf. Hosea 2: 18). 'And the cow and the bear shall feed; their young ones shall lie down together; and the lion shall eat straw like the ox. And the sucking child shall play on the hole of the asp, and the weaned child shall put his hand on the basilisk's den (Isaiah 11: 6-8). The poetic hyperbolism has an underlying idea. This is God's world. Nature can not remain 'red in tooth and claw' under His dominion. The whole universe is His creation and the scene of His activity, the physical part must, therefore, express His nature. He cannot leave it out of His scheme and it cannot be given an existence apart from Him. The Messianism of the Prophets grew out of the desire not only to 'break down the gulf between God and man', but to remove the gulf between God and the world. This larger scope gives a distinctive quality to Jewish Messianism.

The question which exercised the Jewish philosophers of later times, as it exercised other philosophers, whether matter is eternal, could not have arisen in the minds of the Prophets; not only because they were not philosophers but also, perhaps even more, because the dualism of matter and spirit could not have occurred to them. Matter, like spirit, is an integral part of God's creation.

The implications of that idea reach far. By the ultimate reality which is implicitly ascribed to the physical aspect of the universe, it imparts a high intrinsic value to human life on earth. This estimate is expressed in the teaching of Judaism that this life is not merely a preparation for another life, but that it is also an opportunity to express and attain eternal values. So the final judgment will not destroy the world but renew it. The world is permanent, God did not form it to be destroyed. 'For thus saith the Lord that created the heavens: he is God, who formed the earth and made it; he established it, he created it, not a waste, he formed it to be inhabited; I am the Lord, and there is none else' (Isaiah 45: 18). The final judgment will not end human life on earth but change humanity.

The consummation of history will bring the establishment of the Kingdom of God on earth, that is, His rule will be universally recognised and obeyed. It will reveal fully and clearly His righteousness. Therefore, Deutero-Isaiah treats as synonymous the nearness of God's righteousness, and the coming of His victory. His rule, the moral order of the universe, will be fully revealed and justified, when human history attains its destiny.

But how will this consummation be achieved? The answer given by the Prophets presents another paradox in their thought. The social reforms which they demanded and the repentance for which they pleaded, implied that men could set the course of history, that they can co-operate with God to fulfil His purpose for humanity. But the whole framework of the Prophets' thoughts must preclude the idea that 'God's purpose could be fulfilled only through the co-operation of men'.[1] Men evoke God's activity according to their deeds, but the fulfilment of history will be the work of God. In the end, God will overrule men's freedom to do wrong. But that faith did not relieve men and nations of the obligation to further the spiritual and moral progress of mankind by their lives and conduct. A special obligation lay on the people of Israel. The salvation of mankind will come with the universal spread of the true worship of the true God. Israel has been endowed with the function to further the progress of humanity to this spiritual and moral attainment. It has been chosen to serve God and humanity, by bringing the knowledge of God to humanity and bringing humanity to the worship of God.

The logic of monotheism required the recognition of God's rule over all the nations but did not exclude a special position with a special function for one nation. On the contrary, the history of monotheism led naturally to the belief that the Hebrews had such a position. They alone among all the peoples of the ancient world were given the knowledge of the One God. That revelation, which made Judaism a unique

[1] A. B. Davidson, in the article on 'Prophecy' in the *Encyclopaedia Britannica*, p. 116B.

L

religion, made the Jews a unique people. The distinction entitled them to the epithet: 'Chosen People'. They were chosen for the service of God, to be His witnesses. It imposed on them a responsibility not only for their own history but also for the world's history. The Prophets did not isolate the life of their own people from the life of mankind. Humanity was a unit in their thought. Even occasional outbursts of national chauvinism are soon swallowed up in the larger vision. The Hebrews are the centre of the Prophets' world, but the whole world was the basic reality.

The Jews have a mission. That idea, present incipiently in the earliest Prophets, attains its full expression, as the clear sunshine at noon fulfils the process begun at dawn, in the second part of the Book of Isaiah. The conception of the mission did not, however, entail the kind of work now associated with the missionary idea, individuals seeking individual converts. That interpretation of the Jews' mission was adopted, and followed, in later Judaism. The Gospel of Matthew complains that it was pursued too energetically and zealously. But the Prophets' idea of the mission is the collective influence of the Jews on the religious life of humanity. The question: If the Jews have a mission, where are their missionaries, would have been completely irrelevant to their thought. It is occasionally said that individuals will be converted to, or join, the Jewish religion (Isaiah 14: 1, Zechariah 8: 23). But the Prophets' general idea of the mission was not to win individual proselytes to Judaism by the efforts of individual Jews, but to win all peoples for Judaism by the influence of the spiritual and moral qualities in the life of the Jews collectively and of Jews individually. It was the mission to convert the world to monotheism.

The spiritual and moral quality, therefore, in the life of Israel involves, and implicates, the future of mankind. That is why Israel must pay a higher penalty than other peoples for spiritual and moral faults. Her transgressions are all the more serious because they involve a treasonous dereliction in the high service for which God has chosen her. The election, conferred on her by His grace, was a noble privilege, with a correspondingly great responsibility. It does not entitle her to favour; on the contrary, she must suffer two-fold for her sins. 'You only have I known of all the families of the earth; therefore I will visit upon you all your iniquities' (Amos 3: 2). She will not be completely destroyed in the calamity which she certainly will bring on herself by her sins, a remnant will survive (Isaiah 10: 20ff, 28: 5, 37: 31, 65: 8; Ezekiel 6: 8, 12: 16, 14: 22ff; Zephaniah 3: 13). Though at times a prophet declares (e.g. Isaiah 30: 12ff) that the destruction will be complete, the hope that a remnant will survive was necessitated by the general conception of Israel's destiny. God needs it—the remnant—for His witnesses, and for the same reason the whole nation will, after its suffering, be restored spiritually and materially. The physical restoration and the spiritual reformation will attest to the nations the reality of God and the certainty of His rule. 'Then the nations that are left round about you shall know that I the Lord have builded the ruined places, and planted that which was desolate: I the Lord have spoken it, and I will do it;' (Ezekiel 36: 36). Ultimately, non-Jews will be converted to the Jewish religion (Isaiah 2: 3, 14: 1, 19: 18ff; Jeremiah 3: 17, 16: 19f; Zephaniah 2: 11, 3: 9; Zechariah 8: 20ff).

The thought of the Prophets combined universalism and particularism. God is the God of all nations, but

Israel is given a central place in His rule. By the universal religious significance given to the election of Israel, universalism and particularism were harmonized. It put the election into a universal framework. It described the function and destiny of the Jews in human history. On the whole, the doctrine of the election of Israel in the Prophets is rarely marred by national chauvinism. Sometimes a prophet predicted material glory and wealth for the future of Israel; but that expectation occurs rarely and probably at times when the nation suffered oppression or distress. The material blessings accompany, and signify, spiritual and moral attainment. The 'new Jerusalem' will be physically beautiful because it will be spiritually and morally purified. National morality and national prosperity are closely related in the Prophets' thought. The true worship of the true God will bring well-being. In Israel's case the relation draws enhanced importance from Israel's function in God's purpose for humanity.

The Prophets' Messianic hope emerges from the confluence of faith and experience. At the centre of their thought was the absolute assurance that the world was created and is ruled by the one God who is perfect goodness. On the other hand, they experienced, and saw, the evil in the world: unrighteousness, inhumanity, war among men, and the conflicts unto death in nature. The world as it is does not fit the sovereignty of God; the evil in it makes it ungodly. They could not escape from the dilemma by ascribing the evil to a power, or deity, other than God. Monotheism did not allow it. Nor could they deny the reality of the evil by denying the reality of the aspect of the universe which harbours it. They could not say that the state of this world had no ultimate significance, because this world itself had no ultimate reality, that the fullness of God's rule belongs to another world, and that the real significance of human life will be attained in another life. They could not escape from evil into beatific visions of an unearthly life; their horizon was at the boundaries of the experienced universe.

It gives a particular value to the thoughts of the Prophets that it accepts the ultimate reality of this world and the ultimate significance of this life. They had a realistic faith—that is a faith which accepted facts. All that existed in God's universe had a right to be there. They were, therefore, not intellectually aware of a problem of evil. But they were emotionally disturbed, deeply pained, by its existence. The severity and bitterness with which they condemn wrongdoing corresponds to the depth of their pain, and the terrible doom they threaten corresponds to their passionate, impatient, eager longing for the people's repentance. The suffering of the righteous especially burdened their spirit. The doctrine of a 'day of judgment', which would bring to the righteous and to the unrighteous the appropriate consequences respectively of their virtue and sin, eased that burden. And the Messianic hope assuaged the pain caused by the existence of evil. The world is permanent, the evil in it is only temporary. In God's creation it cannot endure, its own consequences will destroy it. The faith and philosophy of the Prophets demanded the fulfilment of God's purpose, the full manifestation, the complete revelation, of His nature and rule in this world. Evil will be destroyed and good established in the consummation of the historic process which is, under the rule of God, destined to fulfil His purpose for humanity. So the Prophets' philosophy of history combines their passionate belief in the universal sovereignty of a God of righteousness and their pained reaction to the evil —personal, social and national—in the world.

The three elements, principles or affirmations in the Prophets' philosophy of history, that it is governed by the moral law, that it will bring 'a day of judgment' and that it will culminate in a Messianic fulfilment, constitute a unity. They are bound together by a common origin in the belief in the universal and comprehensive sovereignty of God, and they are inter-related essentially. Together they give the meaning in human history.

The Prophets' view of history is rejected by the religious philosophy which conceives God as too sublime to be involved in human affairs, and opposed by the materialistic philosophy which places history under the control of economic factors. To the first, the Prophets would have answered that it empties God of life and the world of divine significance. To the second, they would have answered that it degrades man by denying any power to his spiritual and moral endowment. The two philosophies have in common a non-theistic view of human history. The Prophets, on the other hand, saw in it the constant working of God. The historic process belongs to His scheme of salvation for men and mankind.

In their darkest moments, induced by bitter disappointment and frustration, the Prophets sometimes despaired of the human situation but they never lost faith in the ultimate victory of righteousness. Man's share in the historic process is uncertain, but not God's. Therefore, the present is dark, but the ultimate future is bright. The Prophets combined pessimism and optimism; the first applied to the human situation, the second to God's rule. The combination explains the juxtaposition of prophecies of doom and prophecies of hope. Jeremiah saw in his contemporaries no possibility of repentance; they had so habituated themselves to sin that it had become ingrained. Yet the time will come when the law will be written in the hearts of men. Micah's book is heavy with prognostications of doom, but at the end the sky clears and the sun shines forth in the dawn of a perfect day. The contrast is so sharp that scholars have ascribed the last chapter to someone other than Micah. Logically the two atmospheres cannot live together, but psychologically the combination not only fits into the whole framework of the Prophets' thought but is required by it. Theologically the combination of prophecies of doom and prophecies of hope implies the doctrine that God's grace will ultimately, by the working of His law, save mankind from the doom to which its evil must bring it. The Prophets' intense faith in the righteous God and the pain caused by the evil of men produced an explosion into bitter outbursts against men; but behind the bitterness was tenderness, and beyond the impending disasters they saw the salvation of God's love, the rising of 'the sun of righteousness with healing in its wings' (Malachi 4: 2).

If humanity's future depended only on men, there would be no ground for hope; on the contrary there would be too much ground for despair about the future. Men are capable of the blackest cruelty, the vilest inhumanity. Without God there is no reason, only sentimental wishing, to expect good rather than evil. The optimism of the Prophets, which has become the optimism of Judaism, issues from the faith in God's concern for this world and this life. The faith in God can be combined with pessimism about the world only if it is taken out of God's care, thrust, as it were, beneath His notice. Such a view of the world was impossible for the Prophets. To thrust it beneath God's notice would be to push Him out of it. But the belief that He was concerned in this world must mean that it will ultimately fulfil His will and accord with His rule. That will be the Kingdom of God. The moral law, which rules history, assures that ultimately the world will be changed into the better world which God's rule requires.

In the fulfilment of the divine purpose for human history, all the nations will be saved to worship the true God in the true way (Isaiah 2: 2ff, 18: 7, 23: 17, and Chapters 40-45; Jeremiah 4: 2). When God's Kingdom is fully established, His righteousness will be fulfilled in men's righteousness (Isaiah 11: 3, 32: 15). History is under His direction, so that it will lead to the clear and everlasting establishment of His dominion, with life on earth dominated by faith in Him; and, fully conforming to His law of righteousness, it will be blessed with the fruits of righteousness.

GENERAL INDEX

INDEX OF PASSAGES CITED AND REFERRED TO

(*Biblical references are according to the Revised Version*)